SHIP AND SHORE

SHIP AND SHORE
Life in the Merchant Navy

DAVID STEVENSON

CAEDMON OF WHITBY

ISBN 0905355 52 0

CAEDMON OF WHITBY PUBLISHERS
128 Upgang Lane,
Whitby, North Yorkshire

Printed and bound by
SMITH SETTLE
Ilkley Road, Otley, West Yorkshire, LS21 3JP

CONTENTS

LIST OF ILLUSTRATIONS

ABBREVIATIONS

A A	Anti Aircraft
A N D	Admiralty Net Defence
A/S	Anti Submarine
B OT	Board of Trade
C A M	Catapult Aircraft Merchant Ship
D E M S	Defensively Equipped Merchant Ship
D E	Destroyer Escort
L C 1 (P)	Landing craft
L C Q	Landing Craft Quarters
L C M	Landing Craft Marines
L C R	Landing Craft Rockets
L CT	Landing Craft Tanks
L ST	Landing Ship Tanks
M F A	Merchant Fleet Auxiliary
M O W T	Ministry of War Transport
N C S O	Naval Control Service Officer
O O D	Officer on Deck
O O W	Officer on Watch
P A C	Parachute and cable Rockets
P T	Patrol Boats
S O E	Senior Officer of Escort
T B S	Talk Between Ships
T S	Training Ship
V1	German Flying Bomb

ACKNOWLEDGEMENTS

I would like to express my appreciation for the encouragement and advice I have received from Ernest Butler, a professional editor; also Kenneth and Margaret Braim for their invaluable help and most practical assistance with the arduous preliminary work on the typescript (not to mention deciphering my handwriting); thanks to Bernard Nelson for giving me the account of his brother's experience in a torpedo ship; my thanks go also to Cordelia Stamp, whose help in having this book published has so greatly assisted me.

Finally my thanks to my wife Joyce and my daughter Hilary whose love and support are continuous.

1
"THERE'S NO SUCH WORD AT SEA"

I stood at the rail of the main deck, watching the expert approach of the seventeen foot Shetland dinghy. She was a beautiful sight in the August sunshine, with her varnished hull gleaming amber in the sparkling waters of the Clyde Estuary. Just as it seemed that she must ram the great steel hull beneath my feet, she turned sharply into the wind, her white sails came down with a run, and a rope struck me hard across the arm as she fell neatly alongside.

"Make fast, son!" called a voice

"What kind of knot shall I put in it, sir?" I asked.

The Second Officer looked up, his face a study of conflicting emotion. His first words were unprintable but I got the message. A round turn and two half hitches on a stanchion.

I remembered the words of Captain "Jock" Mitchell, the ex-commodore Master of Eagle Oil and Shipping Company.

"Remember son, – at sea there's no such word as can't!"

From a small boy, I had always wanted to go to sea. After several unsuccessful applications to various companies I had finally succeeded, thanks to Captain Mitchell. After a hectic session of B.O.T. eyesight tests, a medical, and several letters, followed by frantic packing, I found myself on board the twelve thousand ton motor tanker *San Conrado*, one of the more modern ships of the Eagle Fleet. She was only a few years old and to me was the finest ship lying at the Tail o' the Bank.

The Second and Third Officers swung aboard, grinning at my discomfiture. Only a few years older than I, yet they had that air of assurance and self-confidence which is the mark of the professional seaman. The Second Mate, in his mid-twenties, was to be decorated later for his part in the famous Malta Convoy. As Chief Officer of the *Ohio* he and the Third Officer, steered the ship from the battened-down tiller flat. At any moment the sorely battered ship could have sunk under them.

The Third Officer was a tall, remarkably good-looking boy of twenty, with a lively sense of humour. He was to rise to be the Marine Superintendent of a great shipping company. But on this August afternoon, both were trying to temper discipline with kindness, to a rather apprehensive new boy.

"Always remember son – a round turn and two half hitches when making fast a boat. Now get a bucket and a mop and give her a good wash-down."

"Aye aye, sir!" I jumped into the dingy, whistling.

"And don't whistle on a ship, son. D'you want to whistle up a gale?"

When I came off watch the following afternoon, the other apprentice, Greener, was preparing the dinghy for a sail. Rather than go below I gave him a hand, envious of his opportunity to sail in the boat. I had climbed out on to the deck when the Second Mate and Third Mate arrived.

"Like to come Stevenson?" asked one of them

"Yes sir."

"All right. Get yourself aboard. Just remember, keep out of the way and – keep your nose down!"

I sat forward with Jack Greener, tense with excitement. The sails previously hoisted, flapped impatiently over our heads. The dinghy danced and tugged at her painter, as if she too were impatient to be off.

The two mates settled themselves in the sternsheets.

"Let go, forrard!"

Jack cast off the painter and with a deft sheer of the helm, the sails filled and we were off on a broad reach across the blue water of the estuary.

The boat was sloop rigged. That is, a leg of mutton main sail, with a gaff and boom, and a jib-sail. She had no keel, but was ballasted with canvas bags full of sand. Her design was that of the local Shetland fishing boats, double ended, and very seaworthy. She was the brainchild of the Marine Superintendent, himself a Shetlander. His idea was to have every ship's officer in the Company capable of handling a small sailing boat. That his idea was a sound one was proved by the many epic voyages made by ships' lifeboats of the Company during the war.

As we tore through the water Greener told me the various functions of the sails and sheets. I absorbed it all like a sponge. Greener repeated the Second Mate's advice.

"When going about, or gybing, keep your head down. There's 150 square feet of sail up there, and when it fills, the boom could knock you overboard as it comes across."

After tea we went out again. This time we were to take the Captain and his wife across to a "Chummy ship", a Norwegian tanker called *Andrea Brovig*, for a social call. Jack was on duty, so, in addition to the Captain and his lady, there were the second and third mates and myself.

We helped Captain Vidot and his wife on to the gangway of *Andrea Brovig*, and went off for a sail, with orders to return in an hour. The Second Mate was doing some fancy sailing; tacking, gybing, reaching, all with the object of getting me into the drill of sailing a boat.

Gybing is the opposite of tacking. Instead of going from one tack to the other by bringing the wind round the bow, one does it by bringing the wind round the stern, a rather more tricky manoeuvre.

We had just completed a gybe. I was tending the sheet of the jib, waiting for the sail to fill, when there was a rattle of blocks, a thud and a splash. The dinghy shot away but almost immediately came up into the wind, shivering like a startled pony.

The Third Mate's face was a study. He was looking round in wonder.

"Where's the Second Mate?"

"There, sir! Starboard side!"

"Blimey!"

The Second Mate was treading water, spouting like a small whale. His cap floated nearby.

"Well, don't sit gawping!" he roared. "Do something!"

Helpless with laughter, we reached out with the boathook, and pulled the spluttering second mate into the boat.

When he had recovered his breath, he said through chattering teeth.

"That's how NOT to do a gybe!"

After he had a brisk rubdown on board the *Conrado*, and a stiff tot, we set off to collect Captain Vidot. The Master's eyes twinkled as he climbed into the boat.

"Been doing some sailing, Second Mate?" he asked drily

There were two apprentices on *San Conrado*. Myself, a first tripper, and the Senior Apprentice, a husky, fair haired lad from Yorkshire. He had been at sea for eight months, and to me he was a hairy old shellback. We shared the "Half-deck", a cabin ten feet by eight feet, on the port side of the bridge accommodation Two fifteen-inch brass ports, polished to perfection, opened over a settee, running along the outboard bulkhead. At each end of the settee stood narrow wardrobes, one for each boy. The inboard bulkhead, after one had entered the door, held two bunks, upper and lower, each with its blue counterpane emblazoned with the symbol of the Company, the Mexican Eagle, which had a more pithy but unprintable title. Drawers were set beneath the lower bunk. On the forward bulkhead was a chest of drawers, over which was a small bookshelf. The after bulkhead held a wash-basin, mirror and bottle-rack. On the floor was a strip of blue-patterned carpet. The woodwork was dark and polished. There was something comfortable about the whole room. For the next several months it would be my home.

"Which bunk d'you want, Steve?" asked Jack. "I'll take the upper. We'll be on watch and watch, six hours on and six off. That's the way the Mate wants it. And he's the boss."

This was rather hard on two young and healthy boys. It meant working on deck or on the bridge during daylight hours. It also meant staying up half the night, when one's body cried out for sleep. But it was excellent training for time-keeping and for learning to sleep at any time, anywhere. To this day I can drop off for twenty minutes or so, and wake up, completely refreshed.

"There is a saying at sea – " said Jack. I was beginning to think there were a lot of 'Sayings at sea', and said so, but Jack went on "Next to a jelly fish, the lowest form of marine life is an apprentice".

This I was beginning to appreciate. Jack continued,

"But don't you believe it. There are four people on board whom you address as 'sir'. That's the 'Old Man', the Mate, and the Second and Third Mates. Anyone else on board, you don't give a damn for. Right?"

It was sound enough advice, but it was to get me into hot water more than once.

Another thing I found hard to take was the answering of "Two Whistles". On the average merchant ship there are not a lot of hands available. The custom is for the officer on watch to call for what he wants, by blasts on his pea whistle.

The signals are: One whistle – Standby man to report to bridge
Two whistles – Apprentice – ditto –
Three whistles – Read the log, aft, and report

It was undignified, somehow, to have to answer whistles rather like a little dog. But when I mentioned this to Jack he pointed out the alternative, which was to remain on the bridge.

So I learned to endure "Two Whistles", but I never liked them.

I had joined the ship before she went to her discharging berth. Two days later she steamed up the Clyde, past Dumbarton Rock to Bowling Oil Terminal, to discharge twelve thousand tons of petrol. The two junior officers now joined Jack and I in our tedious six hour watches. A pumpman from the Engine Room overlooked the huge cargo pumps. The Chief Officer remained in overall charge of the proceedings, in addition to his many other duties. The Captain, remaining in lordly isolation from such mundane matters as cargo, went ashore to the ship's agent to conduct ship's business.

He was a tall dignified figure, with a shock of pure white hair. He looked every inch a shipmaster, and was a popular man in the Company. His wife, a lively, intelligent woman, was given to mothering us boys. This consisted of bringing us sticky cakes and sweets from shore, but had absolutely no effect on our awful "Six on and Six off".

For the first time I saw the effects of alcohol on seamen. It seemed to me that the whole business of signing off the old crew and engaging the new, was conducted in a kind of alcoholic haze. At least, on the part of the crew. The officers were sober, but with few exceptions, the ratings didn't seem to care whether they were on or off the ship.

Apprentices did not sign articles of agreement, but were indentured to the ship owner. These indentures I had signed some weeks before. I was not to frequent "Taverns, ale-houses, or houses of ill-repute."

We sailed from Bowling at 4.0.am on 19th August 1940. I had been on cargo watch from eight the previous evening, until two that morning. I was called out for unberthing from four till six, then found myself on sea watch from eight till two that day. Small wonder that when I came off duty, I crashed into my pit for a blissful caulk.

When I went on watch again at 8.0.pm, the ship was well down the Clyde. All about her in the summer dusk were ships which would form the convoy. To starboard the blue hills of the Kintyre Peninsula stood out in bold relief against the last of the gloaming.

I stood on the bridge, fascinated by all that was going on. The Captain, in duffle coat and short leather sea-boots, was conning the ship, aided by the Third Mate, also duffle clad, with a pair of binoculars slung round his neck. At the wheel stood a seaman, now miraculously sober. I felt a sudden thrill. At last I was at sea.

By next morning the convoy was well out into the Atlantic, with the coast of Northern Ireland just visible as a thin dark line to the South.

The ships had now taken on some sort of order. They steamed in five columns abreast, six ships to a column. Little scraps of bunting flew at their triatic stays, denoting in International Code, their Convoy number. Thus, the leading ship of the centre column in which the Commodore flew his flag, was number 31, the next astern, number 32 and so on. Our number was 43, which meant that we were third in line in the fourth column. Ships were supposed to keep two cables astern of each other, and columns five cables apart. Thus the area of a convoy such as ours would be two miles across, and one to two miles in length. Outside of this on escort duty, roamed two corvettes and a trawler, with an "I" Class destroyer in the van as Senior Officer Escort – S.O.E. They were to protect the convoy from attack from a stealthy torpedo to a pocket battleship.

As the days went past, the crew settled down to the routine of convoy.

One of my duties as darkness fell, was to check the blackout arrangements. I made my way round the entire ship, calling out "Blackout, please, blackout!" Then round a second time to ensure that every cabin and store room had the deadlights secured. This was a very necessary chore. One story was of a destroyer, fed up with a certain uncovered porthole on a cargo boat, putting a blank round through it, which landed at the feet of an astonished fireman just off watch. Be that as it may, I was very careful about blackout.

On the seventh day out, we had reached "Twenty West", the point of dispersal for the convoy.

It was not until much later in the war that convoys were escorted clear across to the States or Canada, to New York or Halifax, N.S. In 1940, at the dispersal point, the convoy broke up, each ship proceeding independently to her destination.

At ten o'clock one fine Autumn morning, the Commodore ship hoisted the flag signal which was the order to disperse. Also hoisted was the International Code signal "W.A.Y." meaning "Goodbye – Good Luck". Then increasing to full speed, she shot ahead, and was soon a speck on the horizon. We watched her go with a touch of envy. A banana boat, she could do sixteen knots.

The remaining ships, more modest in speed, stayed, if not in company, at least in sight of each other for the greater part of the day. One tall funnelled cargo boat, the *Marconi*, seemed to have a similar course to the *San Conrado*. She hung abeam of us all day until darkness fell.

After the break up of the convoy there was a feeling of relief among the crew, a kind of release of tension. The ship was out of the Danger Zone. The weather was warming up, and in another ten days we would be in the West Indies.

Next morning when I went on the bridge to scrub out the wheelhouse, the Captain said sharply

"Leave that, Boy. Get on the starboard wing and keep a sharp lookout!"

"Aye, aye, sir!"

It was only then that I noticed the tenseness of the normally carefree Third Officer. Every few seconds he would sweep the horizon with his glasses. He came over to me.

"The *Marconi* was torpedoed at six this morning. So keep your eyes skinned for a periscope or a torpedo track!"

A cold hand gripped my heart. So much for the "Danger Zone" and the feeling of safety once we had left it. I thought of the terrible explosion in that ship. She could only be over the horizon. The terror and panic of men roused from sleep. It came to me that I knew nothing of the sea. It was suddenly huge and frightening.

At the next opportunity I asked the Third Mate

"Can't we go to the rescue?"

He looked at me. His eyes were bleak

"No, Lad. Our orders are – 'no rescue'. That's what the Navy's for".

"But surely we can do something". I protested.

"Look, Lad, don't you think Jerry will be waiting for just such a thing as a fine fat tanker rushing to the rescue? Be your age, and keep a lookout!"

But the crisis passed, and as the miles slid past under the keel, so did the *Marconi* slide from memory.

As the weather grew steadily more fine, the Mate began to organise "Tank-cleaning" in readiness for the next cargo. A modern tanker has special high pressure steam cleaning equipment for cleaning her cargo compartments. This makes short work of the disposal of oily sludge formed by corrosion and rust mingling with petroleum. But in 1940 sweat, elbow grease, and a high pressure Mate accomplished what high pressure steam does today.

All hands turned out. dressed in the oldest and most worn clothes for "tank-diving". We were issued with wooden pegged tank boots, a small wooden scoop, and a galvanised bucket. These precautions were necessary for one spark in an empty tank, igniting a pocket of gas, could blow up the entire ship.

Most of the sea water ballast having been pumped out during the night, the ship was riding high out of the water. The bosun was busy with two of the hands, rigging jackstays fore and aft on the decks. From these the windsails would be hung, to dip their long canvas snouts into the tanks, pushing air into the ventilation.

The scene was a busy one as the crew swung into the work. Four men went into the tank to be cleaned. Two stayed on deck by the hatch, to haul up and dump the buckets of rust and sludge.

I was one of the "tank-divers". I had received plenty of advice from the A.Bs.

"Soon as your eyes start to prick, come up. 'It's a sure sign you're being gassed' ".

"Never try to rush up on deck if you're feeling dizzy. You'll pass out, sure as death, an' fall off the ladder!"

"Keep your face away from the 'mud'. That's where the real gas lies".

The tank was a huge steel box, some thirty feet square by forty feet deep, one of twenty one such divisions of the ship's hull. A steel-runged ladder led from the tank hatch to the bottom of the ship. The hatch itself was about three feet by two. A tanker has no double bottom, save in the engine room. She is built on a system of longitudinal heavy beams, tied together by deep transverse frames and smaller stiffeners. Known as the "Isherwood System", to all intents and purposes she is a huge box girder. So my tank was a big box, from whose inner surface protruded at intervals, deep frames about two and a half feet wide, on which men could walk.

The steel work was golden brown in the shaft of sunlight coming through the tank hatch. Though it was hard to see from the deck, the bottom was illuminated by a dim but sufficient light, rather like that in a cathedral. From forward to aft, the ten-inch cargo lines ran about eighteen inches above the bottom. In the bays between the stiffeners, steam heating coils writhed like tortured snakes.

It was hot, very hot. It also reeked of petrol fumes.

"Come on Steve, let's get started".

A voice recalled me to the job at hand. It seemed easy. Scoop up the rust, using an old broken broomhead to sweep it into the scoop, fill the bucket, and send it up on the heaving line.

The smell was powerful, heady. The smell of a hundred filling stations rolled into one. Gradually the fumes got into one's lungs, into one's taste buds even; so that to spit was to spit petrol. To swallow was to swallow petrol.

A great exhilaration took hold of me. Presently I began to sing. This was the life. My mates were grand fellows. How magnificently my voice rang in the tank. Why were they looking at me so curiously? I was working, wasn't I? I was merely singing to keep up my spirits. Ha! That's a good one. Keep – up – spirits!

I gagged on the rum, gasping and choking as the fiery liquid ran down my gullet. Then I burped. Ugh! It was all petrol fumes.

"That's the ticket". said a voice. "Have another drop o' rum".

I found myself sitting on deck, my bucket against the hatch coaming. I had passed out in the tank, my lungs full of petroleum vapour. Rum was the only thing which would "break" the wind and release the fumes from my breathing.

"Feeling better now, Son?" asked the Mate.

"Yes, sir". I got to my feet and headed dizzily for the hatch ladder.

"Hey, not so fast, my lad. Take a turn on hauling up the buckets".

It was back breaking work, heaving up the heavy buckets. There was no end to the voices calling from the bowels of the ship. But the fresh air and sunshine were wonderful tonics. By lunchtime I was starving. I had two helpings of plum duff.

But it was not all work at sea. At this stage in the war, shipboard life out of convoy, still ran on peace-time lines. The usual watch-keeping system of "four on and eight off" prevailed. Except in our particular case, as apprentices, of "Six on and six off". After four in the afternoon the first dog watch, from four to six, and the second dog, from six to eight.

The main periods of rest and recreation were in the evening between four and five o'clock we could play deck golf, table tennis, darts or cards, and swim in a canvas pool rigged on the main deck abaft the bridge. Five to six p.m. was tea-time. After tea, until eight p.m. yarning, reading, writing letters, studying, or visiting the engineers who lived aft, even playing musical instruments and ancient gramophones, was the usual form of entertainment. One of the lads had a harmonica. With this, and combs and paper, we would sit out on the saloon deck, under the stars, making what we thought was tolerable music. It was pleasant to sit thus, with the bow wave rushing past in a flurry of broken water, flecked with

I climbed up to the crow's nest to take this picture.

Dhobi time on deck.

phosphorescence, while the ship rolled easily on her way to the Indies.

Saturday afternoons were "Dhobi" days. All our smalls and other clothing had to be washed in a bucket. It was enjoyable to sit in a corner of the deck in the sunshine, slopping one's washing up and down in a bucket of suds, before rinsing, "Blueing", and hanging them out on a stretch of old signal halyard, to flutter briskly in the South East Trade Wind. They were dry by tea-time and Saturday's dog watches were given over to ironing sessions. Some of the results were not up to much. For instance, shirts were ironed according to the rhyme;

> First the cuffs and then the chest,
> Damn and blast all the rest!

We rarely starched our laundry, though I remember one AB who could do a beautiful job, using the water left when the cook had been boiling rice.

On alternate Saturdays, at 4. 0.pm. "Board of Trade Sports" were held. The Merchant Shipping Act of 1896, requires that the crew be mustered for Boat Drill once a fortnight.

The ship's siren would sound the appropriate signal and all hands would proceed to their respective stations, wearing life-jackets. The Muster would be called, the men detailed off, and the boats swung out overside, and re-stowed on their chocks. It was all fairly leisurely. I couldn't help wondering what would happen if we ever had to use the boats in a hurry.

Fire Drill consisted of the whole crew milling round some previously chosen spot, where there was supposed to be a fire. The Apprentices' duty was the Smoke Helmet, The Salvus self-contained breathing apparatus, and the Novita apparatus, a resuscitating oxygen apparatus. The Third Mate was in charge of the equipment. He would rope in some luckless "volunteer" to be encased in the leather jacket and fibre helmet of the Smoke Helmet to stalk about the deck looking like a Martian, clutching in his sweaty hands a fire axe, and a Davey Safety Lamp. Another would be strapped into the "Salvus", complete with artificial lung, to the sarcastic and witty comments of his shipmates, whose turn it would be next time.

Finally a foam fire extinguisher would be solemnly discharged over the side, and handed to the ship's carpenter for re-charging. Thus ended Fire Drill.

Later, on another ship, this chore one day fell to the apprentices. We were allowing the extinguisher to spit cheerfully through a Panama lead, as we thought, into the sea. We were roused from our task by a roar from the flying bridge. The Captain, returning from a visit to the Chief Engineer was staggering along, head down, in a blizzard of flying foam. We had omitted to check the wind direction. Worse, the main deck had been freshly painted the previous day.

After profuse apologies to the Master, we spent the rest of the afternoon scrubbing down acres of steel deck. Fear of the Mate spurred our flagging limbs.

Twenty four hours before sighting land, I could already smell it. It is an exciting, anticipatory scent. After days at sea the lungs and nostrils are completely cleansed of "Shore" smells. So that when the ship nears land, the fresh scent of vegetation is a thrill one never forgets. Some seamen can never "Smell the land", but I have always been able to. Another thing I have always been able to do is to smell fog. It has a salty, fishy kind of smell. Even though the horizon was clear, with no sign of imminent fog, I could say with certainty, "Fog in twenty four hours". Rarely was I wrong.

Next morning *San Conrado* sailed through the Mona Passage, between the islands of Puerto Rico and Hispaniola. There was not much to see since the channel is some fifteen miles wide. But it was good to know we were in the Caribbean Sea.

Thirty six hours later we had made our landfall, the North West tip of Curacao, the largest of the three islands which make up the Netherlands West Indies. These islands, Aruba, Curacao and Bonaire lie off the coast of Venezuala. Aruba, to the West of Curacao is an "Oil island", like Curacao. But Bonaire, to the East, is deserted save for fishermen and some rock salt quarries. Though neither Aruba nor Curacao produce oil, there are large refineries on each, which process the crude oil, brought from Venezuela by a "Mosquito Fleet" of small tankers. These "Jitneys", as they were known, ran round the clock, from the Islands to Lake Maracaibo, in Venezuela. To such exotically named places as San Lorenzo, Batchuquairo and the like. Today, the narrow twisting channel which could only be navigated by the jitneys, has been dredged to take ocean-going tankers, and the large port of Punta Cardon has been built out of what was virtually desert.

Off Willemstad, the pilot came out in a little white motor boat with a large "P" in blue on its bows, and soon *San Conrado* was heading in towards the entrance with her crew standing by at "Stations". There is a fort on the port side of the entrance, and every ship entering or leaving is requested to dip her ensign as she passes. I stood aft, the halyards between my fingers and at a signal from the bridge, slowly lowered the Red Ensign, waited for the Dutch Tricolor to dip in answer, and hoisted it back to the gaff.

A few hundred yards inside there is a pontoon bridge, connecting the two halves of the town of Willemstad, known as Emmastad and of course Willemstad.

The bridge opened to let the ship through, and we were sailing slowly right through the centre of the town. Along the waterfront on either side, lay gaily painted inter-island schooners and fishing craft, brilliant in the morning sunshine. These little vessels trade all over the Caribbean, bringing fruit, salt and people, to and from other islands and the mainland of Venezuela.

Willemstad is neatly laid out in the Dutch Colonial fashion. American cars fill the narrow streets and waterfront, controlled by efficient Dutch policemen at each crossing.

The oil terminal and loading wharves lie round the edge of a large lagoon to the North of the town. This lagoon is called Santa Anna Baai. *San Conrado* tied up at *Bernard Werfe*, so named after the Prince Consort. All the ocean wharves were named rather than numbered. Names like *Emma Werfe*, *Wilhelmina Werfe*, *Oost Pier*, *Oceaan Pier*. All were occupied by tankers, mostly British or Royal Dutch Shell.

That afternoon, the young Radio Operator and I went ashore, travelling down the lagoon and through the Cut to Willemstad by launch or "jitney". I must explain that any small version of any form of transport is known as a "jitney". Thus our motor boat was a jitney, a station wagon would be a jitney, a small coaster would also be a jitney.

We visited "Eddie Cantor's", where a sailor or tourist could buy anything his heart desired and his pocket could stand. "Eddie" was a West Indian with immense business acumen. He had acquired his name from his likeness to the film star. He knew the tanker men of a dozen countries and never forgot a face, and rarely a name. He was very kind to all sailors. I have had the experience of buying from Eddie in peace time, at normal prices, with the shop full of American tourists off the *Mauretania* and Eddie's prices were exactly double. The sign for a Dutch Guilder is "$". Eddie merely stroked through his price tickets again, turning "$" into "$(with two strokes)" – twice the price!

In later years I was to make some good friends in Curacao, but on this, my first trip I didn't know a soul.

On the way back to the ship, our very drunk Second Cook decided it was cooler to swim back. He stepped into the water from the fast moving launch and began to swim up the lagoon. As he had a good mile to go, we shouted to the driver of the jitney to stop. He merely shrugged his shoulders and carried on. Evidently the sight of swimming sailors was a common one to him.

Once on board we looked anxiously back along the lagoon from the poop. No sign of Larry. Then one of the eight inch mooring lines began to sway. In the beam of a torch, Larry could be seen coming up the rope, hand over hand, singing a bawdy song at the top of his voice. He crawled through the rails and oblivious of our presence, staggered below still singing; quite a feat, to swim a mile, then climb eighty feet of rope to the deck of a ship, to say nothing of the singing.

Next morning the ship sailed, bound for Bermuda to pick up a convoy. Outward bound a lot of chipping and scraping had been done. Now that the ship was loaded the decks were only some seven feet above the surface of the sea. So, while it was still fine, all hands got busy painting decks. First the tank coamings were painted a nice shade of grey. Then the tank valves were painted in colours according to their function. Red, blue and green were for Port, Centre and Starboard tank valve wheels. White was for a Master valve, and Buff for a Crossover valve. The overall effect was very trim. The carpenter, once the painting was done, went round each hatch, daubing white lead and tallow on the threads of the wing nuts which secured the tank lids.

It would take us five days to reach Bermuda. Now the Captain decided we must learn to use our gun. This was an ancient 4.7 inch relic of Japanese manufacture. It dated from the First World War and was mounted on the poop. The Second Mate was Gunnery Officer, having had a two-day course in Liverpool. It was his job to choose the gun crew, which numbered six.

Number One was Gunlayer. (Our Senior D.E.M.S. (Defensively Equipped Merchant Ships) Rating)

Number Two was Trainer. (Our Junior D.E.M.S. (Defensively Equipped Merchant Ships)Rating)

Number Three was Swab and Rammer

Number Four was Shell Number

Number Five was Cartridge Number

Number Six was Sight-Setter

I was sight-setter. My position was on the left side of the gun, looking towards the breech. I had two metal dials to set against a pointer, according to the range and deflection called out by the Gunnery Officer.

The Drill would go something like this. There would be a great scramble and scurry as the crew took up their positions.

"Enemy target – Submarine – Bearing Green Five Zero – Range 6000. – Deflection Eight left!"

This was my cue to set the sights.

"Gun's crew – load – "

The breech would be swung open and the shell and charge rammed home. A click as the breech was closed, and the firing pin inserted.

"Aim!"

More fiddling with the laying and training wheels by the Gunlayer, whose duty it was to fire the gun right on the target, an old oil drum thrown overboard for the purpose.

I would turn my face away from the barrel inches from my left ear, and stand with my mouth open to absorb the blast. I must have looked like a fish out of water.

"Fire!"

A terrific detonation beside my head as the gun went off. By turning my head immediately the gun was fired, and sighting along the barrel, I would watch the shell in its flight.

"Splash!"

A great fountain of water would shoot into the air, off the quarter, as the shell landed.

"Down 600. – Deflection 4 Right!"

Once more the gun would boom.

"Check – check – check –!" What had happened now?

The Second Mate was talking to the Rammer.

"Smith, how many times must I tell you to dip the swab and ram into the water bucket? Do you want to blow all of us to Kingdom Come?"

"N'no sir" quavered Smithy.

"Right then. Let's have one last shoot".

Lord knows how we would have fared had we ever met a German warship in those early days. On a subsequent voyage on another ship, the gun was fired while trained on the beam. The detonation jammed all the doors to the engineers' cabins tight shut. It would Take Chippie two days to free them. Still, we had a gun. We could fire it

Bermuda was as lovely as the travel posters depicted it. It is a coral island, with a protecting reef, but evidence of its position in the hurricane tracks was the wreck of a ship, high on the fangs of coral.

The ship was piloted through the reef to the anchorage by a distant relative of mine. He was at once Pilot and Examination Officer. It was intriguing to meet him so far from home, though unfortunately, I was unable to avail myself of his kind invitation to come ashore.

We had the dinghy out again during our stay in Bermuda. It was wonderful to sail in the lagoon in such beautiful conditions. The sun shone. In the background was the green shore of the island. I was rapidly gaining in the skill of handling the boat.

"People pay hundreds to do this. Here we are, getting it all for free!"

After several days we sailed in a convoy of about twelve ships. It was not long before the sunny skies of Bermuda were left behind, and we were in a North Atlantic gale. Four days after our departure, the convoy was due to rendezvous with the main convoy from Sydney, Cape Breton Island. Some time in the afternoon, with rain and spray cutting the visibility to less than a mile, we knew we should be sighting the other ships. We had no Radar to help us. Only our eyes, our senses and our own skilful navigation.

A rain squall darkened the sky. Would we meet the other lot in its drenching gloom? As it lifted, there were the masts and funnels of the main convoy.

Soon we had settled down to the routine of signalling, station-keeping and watching for U-boats.

Each day at Noon, every ship hoisted her position in terms of latitude and longitude, shortly after eight bells. It fell to the officer of the watch and his apprentice to do this, on top of their ordinary duties. In a naval ship there are "Bunting Tossers" whose sole job it is to do the signalling. We had only ourselves and a bridge wing full of coloured flags, waiting to be hoisted to the triatic stay. In a strong breeze it was hard work.

Then came the task of reading the Commodore's flags, and those of our neighbours, to see if the positions corresponded. Some of the old tramp ships waited until several hoists were fluttering in the breeze before hauling up their own, which would invariably be a good average of what was already in evidence.

As the convoy approached St. George's Channel, between Scotland and Ireland, each ship was given its individual destination. This signified the break up of the convoy. As soon as the instructions were de-coded and quick calculations of speed and distance were made, the ships raced off in the effort to catch a favourable tide. A peace-time outlook still existed. The convoy was an inconvenient restriction thought up by some fool in the Admiralty, to be dispensed with as soon as possible. Later, when ships were being sunk, not only in the Western Approaches, but in the Irish Sea and English Channel, convoys were held together right up to the Boom and the Pilot Station.

San Conrado docked in Stanlow, ten miles up the Manchester Ship Canal. It was early October, the weather was damp and miserable. She was going for dry docking and the crew, instead of being paid off on arrival, was retained for tank-cleaning.

One intriguing episode of this trip was the arrest of the 1st Radio Officer, who came from Dublin. During the voyage he had been a great supporter of Hitler and the German people, and many and hot had been the arguments.

As soon as the ship docked he asked the Captain if he could make a flying visit to London for some important personal business. Though late at night, he set off in the blackout and rain. Next morning I was awakened by an Army Security Officer, accompanied by the serious faced Mate.

"Get up, Son. This Officer wants to have a look round your cabin".

The cabins of the radio men and the apprentices, adjacent to each other, were searched most thoroughly. So was the Radio Room. Even the wood panelling was stripped off. All our letters, books

The young cadet.

and personal belongings were scrutinised. The rumour flashed round the ship – Sparks was a spy. As suddenly as it had begun, the searching was stopped. As he left the gangway the Security Officer remarked to the Mate,

"We got him on the London train".

We never saw Sparks again.

Once in dry-dock in Birkenhead the ship paid off and I was sent home on leave to await another ship. What a thrill it was to step out of the train at my home town. How small it looked after the places where I'd been recently.

I was the sailor home from the sea. In my brassbounder uniform, I swaggered round the town. The girls thought I was wonderful.

2
"THE IDES OF MARCH"

I joined M.V. *San Cipriano* on a dismal November day in 1940. She lay in her berth at Stanlow, her vast black hull towering over the dank flatness of the tank farm, red boot topping streaked with rust. The Chief Officer was brusque.

"This is one of the Company's best ships. You have a reputation to keep up. Plenty of work"

I found I was Senior Apprentice, the other boy being a first tripper. We relieved two lads just out of their time. How I envied them "Going up" for Second Mate.

The Mate was as good as his word. No two boys got through more hard graft and long hours than we did. Not only did we do bridge watches, four on and four off, but we were also on gun lookout watches during the night hours. In all we were on duty for sixteen hours out of the twenty four. Apprentices have no Union.

Had it not been for the kindness of the D.E.M.S. ratings, who allowed us to cat nap in the funnel casing from time to time, we would have been out on our feet. I shall always remember the hot acrid smell of the inside of a motor ship's funnel.

We left in convoy as on the previous trip. The weather was foul. A real South-west gale. At about six on the second morning, there was a tremendous crash, and the whole ship trembled. Had we been torpedoed? There was no smoke or cordite fumes, but *San Cipriano* was not answering her helm. There came a call from the engine room.

"The steering gear has gone!"

It had gone all right. The six-inch hydraulic rams which moved the rudder stock had snapped like seaside rock. Even the huge casting which was the frame of the gear, was lying in two pieces on the deck of the tiller flat. The telemotor fluid, a mixture of glycerine and water had run out and men slid around helplessly in the slippery mess now covering the steel plates.

"Rig the jury steering gear", ordered Captain Highley.

We set to work. I was put on bridge duty with the Second Mate. It was my first real storm at sea. I stood, bracing myself against the long deep rolls of the ship as she wallowed broadside to the tremendous seas. I watched the flying spray and foam streaks on the rollers which marched on us in endless succession out of the South-west. The Second Mate tried to signal one of the ships of the rapidly scattering convoy with the Aldis Lamp, but our motion was so severe that he could not keep the lamp focussed on the other's bridge.

Within the hour, the Chief Engineer was lying in the ship's hospital, his elbow smashed and his shoulder dislocated. He had been standing ready to drop a link pin into place, when the tiller swung across and pinned his elbow against the jury sheaves. As it did so, his feet slid out from under him on the glycerine, and he fell. Being held by the elbow, his shoulder joint came out.

It took all hands under Captain Highley's inspired guidance the remainder of that awful day, before the jury wires were rigged up through the sheaves in the poop deck to the mooring winch. By this time the ship had drifted before the gale some twenty miles to the North East. At 2.30 p.m. the black towering crags of the Mull of Oa were only five miles under the lee.

Slowly the big tanker answered her helm, until her bows pointed to the Southward. The after steering binnacle had been torn from its place on the poop by a sea. It was found in the port lifeboat. We salvaged the compass bowl, and rigged it up near the docking telephone, in the upturned legs of a potted palm from the Smoke-Room. It meant continual 'phoning from bridge to poop, checking compasses and giving helm orders to the men of the jury winch on the deck below. We steered an erratic but determined course for Belfast Lough, through a bitter winter night, and slid past Mew Island Light at 3.0 am next day. The Chief was taken off to hospital in Belfast by breakfast time. What was it Captain Mitchell had said?

"There's no such word as 'Can't' ".

We lay at anchor in Belfast Lough for several weeks, awaiting a vacant dry-dock. No one had any proper knowledge of what had caused the accident. The general opinion was that it had been a big sea, or we had "sat" on submerged wreckage.

During our spell in the Lough, Christmas 1940 came and went. My first Christmas at sea. The saloon was decorated with flags. We typed out Menu Cards and decorated them with coloured drawings of holly and robins.

Christmas morning was a fine, clear day. Nearby lay another tanker, MV. *Gretafield*. Full of goodwill, we signalled greetings to her by Aldis lamp. No one answered. Since it was 7.0.am perhaps it was a little early.

I have spent many Christmases on board ships. All but three in twenty years, to be exact. I have eaten turkey and plum duff in a temperature of 104 degrees. I have eaten my Christmas dinner on deck, while standing by to start cargo.

But in Belfast Lough on that first Christmas, the fun was good, the food and the fellowship just fine. We all ate too much. Some of us drank too much. Everyone sang too much. We were hoarse for days afterwards. But we had a jolly fine Christmas.

New Year, a few days afterwards, was not so boisterous, but sixteen bells were rung on the Fo'c'sle bell at Midnight, eight for the Old Year, eight for the New. What it would bring no one could know.

On 4th January 1941, four tugs towed *San Cipriano* down the three mile Victoria Channel, to Harland and Wolff's big Alexandria Dry-dock. Having just had a spell of leave, I was not allowed to go home again. I didn't mind. Belfast in 1941, just before it was blitzed, was a gay place to enjoy oneself. Plenty of dances, cinemas, restaurants, girls.

We got in tow with several of the nicest girls I've ever met. Real Irish charmers. One was a Wren Officer who became the Second Mate's special girl. A succession of parties, dances and social functions followed. It was wonderful. So far as we were concerned, Ulster lived up to its reputation for hospitality. As "Servicemen" we could ride the length of the tramway system from Dundonald to Bellevue for a penny.

There were nights aboard too, when one had to do duty. One rainy night, cries for help were heard coming from aft. Grabbing my torch, I dashed along aft to investigate. From the sounds of splashing, I felt sure someone had fallen into the Lagan. What I found was something different. Our ship was moored outside a ship not yet complete, whose scupper holes had not been cut in her sheer strake. About six inches of water had collected on her decks in the vicinity of our gangway, reached by planks laid to keep our feet dry. One of the firemen returning from a carouse, had slipped off the planks and fallen face down in the water. Thinking he was in the river, he was swimming like made, yelling for help every so often. By his side, propped up against the rails was his mate, mumbling,

"S'all ri' George. Keep swimmin'. I'll fetch a lifebelt in a minute!"

On my first trip I learned that ranks and ratings have their own nomenclature, more piquant than that laid down in the Articles of Agreement.

The Captain whether he be thirty or sixty, is the "Old Man". The Chief Officer is "The Mate".

Second and Third Officers are "Second Mate" and "Third Mate". Only the Chief Engineer is the "Chief", as only the Second Engineer is the "Second". The remaining engineer officers are known by their numbers. e.g. Third, Fourth and so on. The Petty Officers too, have their own titles. The Boatswain is "Bose", the Carpenter "Chips" or "Chippy". The Lamptrimmer is "Lamps" and the Pumpman is "Pumps", while the radio officer is "Sparks'.

The Engine room Storekeeper, who performs a similar role to the Bosun, in the Engine Room department is "Stores". The Cook is universally known as "Doc", and the Chief Steward is "The Steward".

A merchant ship's crew is divided into three departments. The Deck Department is under the Mate, the Engine room Department comes under the Chief Engineer and the Catering Department under the Steward.

Other common shipboard terms are : – Forrard – the fore part of the ship. Midships – the middle part of the ship and Aft – the stern part of the ship. The Flying Bridge on a cargo vessel is a lighter structure sometimes built directly over the wings of the Bridge proper, but in a tanker it is the name given to the Long fore and aft gangway, running from the full length of the decks. Known in American ships as the Catwalk.

The Monkey Island, an intriguing name, is given to the upper bridge or compass platform. I can only conclude that, when the first steamships made their appearance and the top bridge was the only bridge, the sailing ship men scornfully referred to the officers pacing the bridge as "Monkeys". Hence the name.

At last it was time to leave Belfast, on a snowy morning in early February 1941. We had to dig the snow away from the bollards to make the tugs fast. As the ship headed out into the Lough I looked back, a trifle wistfully. Belfast had been kind to us.

Once more it was convoy. More shipping was being sunk and the escorts were much more strict about blackout, station-keeping and smoke producing. Throughout the day a two flag hoist fluttered from the Commodore ship at frequent intervals. "SN – Make less smoke". There were strict orders not to dump rubbish during the hours of daylight. This time the convoy was escorted to 25 degrees West Longitude. What this meant in terms of misery to the crews of the plunging little corvettes, can only be imagined. Two to three more days of freezing cold, of bad weather and sea-sickness, of living on bully beef sandwiches and the interminable naval "Kai", (cocoa to you and me). A corvette, whose design is based on that of a deep sea whale catcher trawler, was a very seaworthy craft. But she was hardly sea kindly. She shipped a lot of water in the waist of the ship, which inevitably found its cold soaking way below decks. On the merchant ships men could be and often were, cold, wet, and miserable. But they all had reasonable accommodation and warm dry bunks in which to sleep. The corvette crews, on the other hand, lived in a hellish existence of bleak deck watches and damp, condensation soaked hammocks, in weather conditions which at best were rough, at worst; appalling.

San Cipriano's destination was Aruba, N.W.I. This was the Western Island of the group, some fifty miles from Curacao. She berthed in San Nicolaas, the main oil port of the island and began to load 80 Octane petrol. At the next berth lay a Shell tanker, M.V. *Eredona*, also loading 80 Octane.

Senior apprentice on the *San Cipriano*.

San Nicolaas and the Capital, Oranjestad, some miles away, were very similar to Willemstad. Indeed it was hard to tell which island one was visiting, as the streets and squares had that unmistakable atmosphere of "Dutch Colonial" about them.

In 1941 80 Octane was a high power petrol, suitable for the fighters and bombers of the Royal Air Force. We were to get an idea of this power unleashed, later in the voyage.

Eredona left some twelve hours before we did. Not that it mattered that much, for we would both join the same convoy from Bermuda.

Though the Mate of the *Cipriano* worked the apprentices hard when in convoy, he had us on day-work for the rest of the trip. We did a lot of scraping of rusty patches on bulkheads and decks, a lot of painting and a reasonable amount of more interesting things. Sewing canvas dodgers and checking and maintaining the stores and gear in the lifeboats. This last was most vital, since the war had become more serious. Up to 1939, ship's lifeboats had merely been things which had to be painted once in a while. They set off a shipshape boat deck. Although by law, Boat Drill was supposed to be regularly carried out, there was many a merchant ship whose lifeboats were so painted up in the chocks that to move them was almost impossible.

In 1934 a steamer called the *Trevesa*, of the Hain Steamship Company, St. Ives foundered in the Indian Ocean. Her Captain and Officers divided the crew into two boats, with the Captain and Third Officer in the other. They took plenty of condensed milk, fresh water and other stores and instruments of navigation. They sailed 1700 miles to reach Mauritius twenty four days later. No life was lost.

This was an historical and praiseworthy voyage in the annals of seafaring. Yet some of the feats of sailing and endurance made by ordinary merchant seamen, between 1940 and 1945 put it completely in the shade. Thirty days, sixty days, eighty days by Widdicombe and Tapscott in a jolly boat and a hundred and thirty five days by a Chinese seaman on a life raft, became, if not commonplace, at least to be expected.

To return to our lifeboats. We checked all the gear. Mast, oars, sail, water – the list was comprehensive. Then came the extras supplied under M.O.W.T. Regulations for war time. Pemmican, chocolate, malted milk tablets, flares, first aid kits, fishing lines. Even a sea water distilling apparatus. Under the Third Mate, we spent a good deal of time checking and seeing that all was in order, should we have to use the boats. One "Comfort" which Eagle authorised to be put in the boats was a box, containing a bottle of rum, 500 cigarettes and matches, sewn up in canvas and painted to make it waterproof and thief proof. Yet one lifeboat which had to make use of this comfort, found that the rum was – cold tea! The remarks of the unfortunate crew, cold, wet, in a bobbing lifeboat, must have blistered the ears of whoever had been responsible for such a shabby trick. It was early March 1941, when "San Cipriano" left Bermuda for U.K. in company with Eredona, Diloma, British Sincerity and Robert F. Hand. All were tankers from the West Indies, bound for England with valuable petroleum of various kinds.

In a few days we had joined the main convoy which had come this time from Halifax, N.S. With our convoy numbers flying we each got "fell in" to our respective stations.

There had been an erroneous impression since the war that tankers and "valuable" ships were placed in the centre of the convoys for maximum protection. I must say I never got this impression in five years of convoys. In this convoy Eredona was given number 12, second ship in the port outside column. Diloma became 23. Our number was, as on my first outward convoy, number 43.

Out of a total of thirty six ships, no fewer than fourteen were oil tankers – a high proportion. The Commodore ship was Elders and Fyffes' Tortuguera, another banana boat.

"Commodores must like banana boats!" remarked the mate morosely. "You'll never catch them on a bleedin' tanker".

Actually he was being hard on the naval officer who was Commodore. The reason for his choice of a passenger/cargo vessel was the extra accommodation in which he could house his staff.

Two days later the convoy was doing "Emergency Turns". These were zigzags of course, executed by flag signals from the Commodore.

Thus, the flag hoist "S.45" meant "All ships turn simultaneously to Starboard" and "P90" meant "All ships turn to port, ninety degrees".

After a few of these, the state of the convoy can be readily imagined. In a naval squadron on manoeuvres, the columns of ships were usually of one class, say destroyers, with similar speeds and handling characteristics. Or battleships which, if not of similar tonnage, at least had the reserves of power needed for manoeuvring. In convoy, there were 4,000 ton cargo liners from the Mediterranean Trade; 12,000 or 15,000 ton tankers, either single or with twin screw; together with fast meat traders from the South American or Australian run. All put in columns and expected to zigzag all over the ocean at a given signal. It was by sheer good seamanship and a modicum of good luck, that within two hours of the emergency turns being finished, the convoy was once more reasonably compact. Darkness fell and with it a fine rain. There was much speculation as to why we had done so much "larking about", and at the amount of signalling which had gone on between the S.O.E. and his corvettes.

We had not long to wait to find out.

The sound of an underwater explosion, whether it be torpedo, mine, or depth charge, is a heart quickening thing, to be experienced rather than described. It is a giant hammer, ringing through the very fabric of the ship, a reverberating clangor whose hollow boom finds an echo not only in one's brain, but in one's bowels.

The attack started on 14th March 1941 – the "Ides of March". The first torpedo struck at 10.10 p.m. to be followed immediately by the second. Both found their mark in Number 12, the Eredona. Within seconds she was an inferno, as twelve thousand tons of high grade petrol roared into the night sky, illuminating the whole convoy in a ghastly red glare which must be seen for scores of miles. Two hundred feet into the air, the flames bellowed in ravening fury. A tanker's masts were roughly one hundred feet and the fire was twice the height of the mastheads. No one, nothing, could survive such a holocaust. The sea for hundreds of feet around Eredona was a mass of flames. On the bridge of Cipriano we watched, in awe-stricken horror. I could not stop myself from trembling. I felt sick at the thought of what must be going on over there.

"Pray the Lord it'll be quick for them!" said Captain Highley.

Eredona fell astern as her engines and her engineers died. Wafted on the light Westerly breeze came the sickening smell of burning petrol, mingled with other things. Somewhere on the deck below, a steward, who had been torpedoed twice before, sobbed in anguish, as slowly the other ships steamed past their stricken companion. The sight steadied me a little. They seemed so steadfast, so full of purpose as they drew away into the darkness, leaving *Eredona* to be her own funeral pyre.

All hands were at Action Stations by now. I took my place as Number 6 gun crew on the poop. It was cold. God, it was cold!

What were the escorts doing? Why were they not depth-charging? Why, oh, why, wasn't somebody doing something? We had no idea how difficult it was to stalk a submarine.

At 10.40 p.m. another resounding clang rang through the ship. Another tanker, *Franche Comte*, this time on our starboard beam. She didn't burn much. Only ghostly blue flames flickered from her fore deck, as she too, fell astern. We stood by till dawn. Nothing more happened. Stiff with cold and delayed reaction, we retired to bed.

Next day the conversation was of nothing else but the events of the previous night.

"The Navy couldn't have got that U-boat. He'll be back". was the general opinion. It was with some apprehension that we again faced the coming night.

At Ten O'clock a ship again was torpedoed. I was called from my station on the gun to relieve the helmsman. I ran along the flying bridge, feeling my toes curling in the anticipation of a torpedo. It was like running on eggs.

As I entered the dark wheelhouse I heard the sound of sobbing.

"Oh, Mother – I want my Mother!"

The helmsman, a young Ordinary Seaman, was in a ghastly state of nerves.

"We all want our Mothers tonight lad" said the Old Man, "Meanwhile you'll have to make do with a smoke. Lay aft and report back here in fifteen minutes!"

I took the wheel, wishing I was on the poop. Here on the bridge we were sitting right on top of the middle of twelve thousand tons of petrol. At least on the poop we were a hundred feet away from direct contact. Maybe I was just kidding myself.

On, through the menacing darkness, the convoy made its slow, steady progress. There were only four people on the bridge, the Captain, Third Officer, a lookout man and myself. It was an eerie sensation to think that unseen eyes might even now be lining up *San Cipriano* in the crosswires of a periscope. I cursed under my breath. It was awful to feel so helpless.

An hour later, instead of the fifteen minutes I had expected, I was relieved at the wheel, and returned thankfully to my place on the poop. It was alive with crew members, dressed for the cold. Each man had his little "Panic-bag," containing perhaps an extra jersey, socks, cigarettes, and sweets

"Wharoom!" Who'd got it this time? On the far side? Another tanker! Gosh! Jerry's sure after the "Oilers"

Within twenty minutes, a further three ships received their death-blows. The escorts were firing star shell, giving a brilliant glare to the scene. Depth charges clanged at intervals.

"What the hell are they lighting us up for? – like bloody Blackpool Illuminations!"

A cry from the Bosun on the port boat deck, "Torpedo to port!" I glanced over the stern. Running past at an acute angle, was the white bubbling wake of a torpedo. He had missed, but only by yards!

An explosion so vast, so stunning that it threw all of us to the deck – an eyeball searing flash that left the men groping and blinded. Surely this time it had been our turn. As my eyes regained their sight, I kept wondering when *San Cipriano's* decks would erupt in flames. Would it really be a quick end?

A cry of amazement came from a dozen throats. I followed pointing fingers. Where the *Joseph H.White* had been following us two cables astern there was now nothing.

"She was carrying Ammo" breathed the Second Mate, his voice an awed murmur.

The telephone from the bridge tinkled. Its message was terse.

"Sub on port beam!"

"Gun's crew – Action!" roared the Second Mate, and seconds later, as we closed up,

"Open sights!"

This meant that the range was too short to set. The submarine must be very close.

"Stand by, lads. Here he comes".

Two cables off, the star shell glare revealed the big long whalelike shape of a U-boat's hull, sliding past, bows cocked up at an angle. She must have been doing ten knots when the depth charges had erupted beneath her, blowing her to the surface. Now her crew fought desperately to bring their ship under control.

"Fire" Our shell hit the water near the U Boat and did a screaming ricochet over the bridge of a Norwegian tanker, in direct line of fire beyond the U-boat.

"Check! Check! Check!" called the Second Mate, then "Cease fire". We daren't fire again. We might hit that ship!

Round our stern swung the S.O.E's destroyer, guns blazing. Her crew had no qualms about shooting.

Blam! Blam! Blam! Three quick shots from her forward guns scored direct hits on the canted bows of the submarine. The Second Mate was prancing with glee, his binoculars glued to his eyes.

"Have a look Steve! Quick! He handed me the glasses. I saw the U-boat roll over, her bow rising vertically into the air. Then she was gone, her farewell a big soft bubble of oily water. How we cheered that destroyer. It was later that I thought of the men in the U-boat. Men, just as frightened, probably, as we were. Men doing their duty, just as we were. My head ached. The problem was too much for me that night.

In the morning, five ships were known to be sunk. Others, deciding that it might be better to go off on their own, had beat it. Thus the convoy, with about a dozen ships less in its ranks, had a rather decimated look. *Diloma*, *Robert F. Hand* and *British Integrity* were still with us plus a couple of Norwegian tankers.

During the day, the S.O.E. steamed through the columns. On her quarterdeck, drawn up in rough ranks and doing half-hearted physical jerks, were some twenty German sailors. The metallic voice of the Tannoy raucously intoned.

"These are some specimens we picked up last night, three U-boats were sunk".

Seven ships for three submarines. A fair score. Our escorts had
done magnificently. Two destroyers and three corvettes, against what
was one of the first "Wolf Pack" attacks of the war. We had no
more trouble, the remaining U-boats having retired to lick their
wounds, and no doubt plan fresh attacks. But not on us.

In years to come I met a friend in my home town who had been
in the Navy during the war. Naturally we got talking about our
adventures on the Atlantic. Comparing notes we found that in the
Eredona convoy attack one of the destroyers *Vanoc*, on which he had
been a signal man, had sunk a U-boat by ramming it and the
Commander, Joachim Schepke, was crushed in his conning tower.
The second U-boat sunk by destroyer *"Walker"*, was commanded
by Otto Kretchmer, who was rescued and in the post war years of
the "new" German Kriegsmarine, became an Admiral.

San Cipriano steamed into the Mersey on a glorious Spring
morning. The scent of fresh green foliage on the Canal banks, as
we proceeded slowly up to Stanlow, was the more vivid for our
recent experience. A heightened joy of living was suddenly ours.

As we started Discharge, the Second Mate said to me,

"Your last ship was the *Conrado*, wasn't it?"

"Yes, sir".

"She was bombed and sunk last week in the Bristol Channel".

I stood, shocked by the news. I thought of Captain Vidot, of Jack
Greener, of all the others I had sailed with.

"How many lost?" I asked.

"Don't know, most of them got out. Young Greener is in hospital
with a bullet in his lung!"

I got the full story much later in the war. A convoy of six tankers,
bound for Avonmouth and Swansea, after a perilous Atlantic voyage,
had been attacked by a flight of Heinkels and Ju 88s within sight
of their final ports. With only the scant protection of an armed
trawler, and their own pathetic Hotchkiss machine guns, it had
been an absolute picnic for the Germans. So low had they been
flying to drop their bombs that the latter, instead of hitting the
ship with their nose fuses, had skidded along the decks and dropped
over the side to explode in the water. The last ship of the convoy, a
British Tanker, had made a gallant attempt to reach the safety of

Milford Haven. But the bombers got her right in the entrance, at the last of the daylight. Six ships, a total of 70,000 tons of petroleum were lost, right on the doorstep.

Would we win the war at this rate?

San Cipriano's next two trips were uneventful. She never returned to Bermuda, Halifax having become the main convoy port for the North Atlantic. Bedford Basin was the ideal anchorage, and could accommodate hundreds of ships. It was well protected by the Narrows, the channel leading between Halifax and the town of Dartmouth on the other side.

With all those ships needing stores, with their crews seeking rest and relaxation, Halifax was transformed in the space of a few months, from a quiet, shabby Canadian small town, to a rip-roaring boom town. Barrington Street rang to the sounds of a dozen languages, as Poles, French, Scandinavian and British seamen strolled and rolled their way up and down its long slope. The "Green Lantern", a kind of Soda Fountain cum Restaurant was the favourite haunt of apprentices, perhaps because the waitresses were younger and better looking than in the other places. The food was good, and a welcome change from shipboard food, which though wholesome, could become monotonous. We enjoyed Canadian hospitality, and bought such things as butter, sugar, tea to a limit of 5 lbs. per commodity, to take to our families back in England.

Around this time, German raiders were becoming active; prowling the Atlantic wastes, in an attempt to destroy whole convoys. One of the company's vessels, the *San Demetrio* was shelled and set on fire by the *Admiral Scheer*, in what came to be known as the *Jervis Bay* convoy in mid-March 1942.

A new procedure was adopted to combat this fresh menace. Two convoys sailed at a fifty mile interval. Each had her Armed Merchant Cruiser, while between the two, patrolled one of our older battleships of the *Royal Sovereign* class. No one, of course, saw fit to tell the merchant crews of this development. One rainy afternoon, a squall lifted to reveal to my startled eyes the outline of a big battleship, well down on the horizon. She was signalling with her searchlight. With thoughts of another *Jervis Bay* episode, I rushed into the wheelhouse where the Second Mate was keeping station.

"A warship – a big one, sir!" I spluttered.

The Second Mate was out of the wheelhouse like a shot, to take a long careful look, through the telescope. He turned to me, grinning as he folded the telescope.

"Relax son – it's one of ours".

Sure enough, it was the *Resolution*.

"Hood and Bismarck"

On that return from Halifax in May 1941 our convoys were about 1,000 miles on our way home. The news was received every six hours from B.B.C. on a particular wave length. On May 24th at about 6.00.am *HMS Hood* was struck by a plunging shell by *Bismarck* which penetrated her magazine and the wonderful pride of the Royal Navy was blown up, losing her entire crew of well over 1,000 men except three survivors. This happened in the Denmark Strait almost halfway between Greenland and Iceland. We knew that we could only be a few hundred miles from this disaster, and could we be the next target? We also wondered if *Bismarck* could have the company of *Tirpitz*.

On that trip H.M.S. *Prince of Wales* sailed right through the convoy from astern. Later we learned that Mr Churchill had been on board. I like to think that he asked to see one of his convoys actually at sea.

On my next voyage I developed appendicitis, shortly after leaving the West Indies. It was not too severe, and after arrival in Halifax, I was examined by a naval surgeon who came on board to see me.

"Grumbling appendix" he said, "D'you want it removed here, or at home?"

I said I preferred to go home.

"Right If the worst comes to the worst, we can always transfer you to the A.M.C."

Though how this was to be done in the stormy Atlantic I have often wondered.

"Can he work?" asked the Mate.

"Yes – light duties only" and the Commander was gone.

Next morning I was scrubbing out the wheelhouse and chartroom. Light duties. Huh!

I was paid off *San Cipriano* in Swansea, in August 1941 and travelled home by train, standing all the way. By the weekend I was in the local hospital, minus one appendix.

The next voyage of *San Cipriano* was to Murmansk. She got a bomb in her galley, which set fire to the cordite in the Ammunition locker. Her Second Mate and an apprentice went down into the choking fumes, and threw all the cordite overboard. On her return to the Tyne for repairs, she was used as a model for the film *San Demetrio, London*.

3

FROM AMERICA TO E-BOAT ALLEY

In December, 1941, I was sent to join M.V. *San Amado* lying in the Thames. She was of similar size and type to my previous ship, but was several years older. The "Half-Deck" was much smaller, with two ports looking aft along the length of the main deck. A main steam line ran through the 'tween deck, immediately beneath our feet making the cabin an oven in the tropics, but very cosy in cold weather.

This time the ship was routed to "Halifax for orders", which was unusual. But once we had left the convoy for some days, we were ordered to proceed to Texas. Since the ship had only bunkered for Halifax, this meant she would have to go into some port on the American Seaboard for bunkers. Excited at the prospect, we ran a sweep on the result.

It turned out to be Port Everglades, on the Florida coast, only a few miles from Miami.

"Marvellous! Just the Job! Now we'll see how the millionaires live!"

Pearl Harbour had just been bombed. America was on our side, really in the war at last.

And, just as we did in 1939, they were making a terrible hash of it. We approached Port Everglades, on a glorious tropical day, flying our International Signal Letters. This is a four flag hoist, such as GFAV, which, when looked up in Lloyd's List, gives the name of the ship. We also flew "G", meaning "I require a pilot" and "Q", meaning "My vessel is healthy and I request free pratique". On our Aldis lamp we were also signalling our name in Morse, to the Coastguard cutter acting as guard ship.

Perhaps it was rather a lot for a raw crew to cope with at once. The signalman of the cutter was very bad at reading. He kept sending

"Repeat please", till I thought the Old Man was going to burst. In the event, the Pilot boat deposited the pilot on board and we steamed past the Coastguard vessel, still flashing "Repeat please". The pilot was laconic.

"These boys sure like to play sailors".

San Amado berthed in a dock reserved for molasses tankers, and we discovered she would be there for twenty four hours. This was wonderful news, but the Mate had other ideas of how to fill the time of the apprentices. Painting the lifeboats!

From this we were saved by being asked to report to the Master. We were introduced to a Mr Elliot, a dark, stocky Scot, who had called to take the "Boys" ashore for a spell. We waited with baited breath for the Captain's decision.

"Mr Elliott, here are the two boys. Are you sure you want them?"

"Oh, yes sir". Mr Elliott's voice was warm, persuasive.

"Right. See you behave yourselves, you two. Look lively now. Don't keep Mr Elliott waiting"

In ten minutes we had bathed and changed and were in the back of Mr Elliott's car, heading out of the dock gate.

"Where do you come from, boys?" he asked, as he drove skilfully through the traffic of the dock area and turned on to the main highway.

"I come from Dunfermline in Scotland" I said.

"I'm from Grimsby in England" said my shipmate.

"Well now, whadda ya know!" Mr Elliott was obviously pleased. "I'm from Aberdeen!"

"I've spent many a holiday there". I responded, and so we fell to reminiscing as the car whirled us through Fort Lauderdale, a beautiful suburb of Miami Beach. Some ten miles from that famous city, it is more quiet and select than its big sister. Palm trees lined the streets and avenues. Beautiful girls and handsome, sun-bronzed men strolled the sidewalks. Set back from the street were lovely homes. We swung round a corner, on which stood the nicest house we had seen so far. The car pulled into the drive way.

"Here we are!" Mr Elliott jumped out and we followed him up the steps. I caught the azure glint of a swimming pool behind a pergola.

"Mother I'm home. I've brought the boys".

"Be right with you. So nice to have you with us again!" called Mrs Elliott. She came through from the kitchen, a small, attractive woman in her late thirties. We were rather puzzled by her remark, but Elliott was quick to explain.

"These aren't your boys this time, Mother. But they're no less welcome". He went on. "Usually we have the boys from the molasses tankers – you know – Athel Line. When I heard there was a ship in the dock, I just assumed it was an Athel Boat".

We were made to feel at home. There was a scrumptious meal, at which we were introduced to the Elliott children. George, a boy of seventeen and Helen a typical American bobby-soxer.

"Now", said Mr Elliott when we had finished the meal. "How would you lads like to go to a real, honest-to-goodness Barn dance?"

We looked at each other.

"Would we?" we chorused. "Just lead us to it".

The dance was held in the Community Centre, a large building in Lauderdale, a combination of dance hall, library, sports rooms and social centre. There were lots of pretty girls and lots of motherly American ladies. There was coffee, doughnuts and coke, and music, and a caller for the dances. I had never been to a barn dance in my life, but I danced every dance. Each time I spoke to a partner, the same thing happened.

"You're from Scotland! My grandmother was Scotch!"

It seemed that every American I spoke to had a Scottish grand parent! Girls came up and got us to autograph their charm bracelets. We felt like a couple of film stars.

It was after midnight when we got back to the house. Mr and Mrs Elliott had gone home before us. Young George drove us, with his girl's head on his shoulder. In the back seat we too had our girls.

"Like to see Dad's boat?" he asked.

"Sure thing, Bing". We were beginning to feel like Americans.

George drove us to the Marina, filled with boats of all kinds, all glossy and shining in the moonlight. He pulled up beside a gleaming forty-footer.

"What a beaut!" I breathed.

Testing the bosun's chair – all 18 stone of him.

"We're going up the Everglades tomorrow for a barbecue. Like to come?"

Would we not? But alas, we would be on the high seas tomorrow bound for Texas.

I was in a bosun's chair next morning, painting the draft figures on the stem, when a car drew up on the wharf.

"Say, David, can you come up a minute?".

On the quay stood Mr Elliott, George, Helen and our two girl friends of the previous evening.

"Got a few things for you" said Mr Elliott.

He dived into the trunk of the car. Eric and I were staggered. Piles of magazines, candy and a home-baked cake from Mrs Elliott. How could we thank our hosts? Sadly we waved farewell from the poop, an hour later, as the ship left Everglades. Would we ever return? We sure hoped so.

Texas City was a small neat city.

One finds that each country has its characteristic smells. India for example, smells of curry, ghee and joss sticks. Iran smells of oil and burning camel dung, Egypt, of bad drains and perfume. England smells of smoke, beer and petrol. America smells of petrol fumes, perfume and cigars – a heady mixture, indeed!

Once loaded, we were soon dropping the pilot off Galveston. A fast, fifteen thousand ton tanker passed, flying the "Stars and Bars". On her bows a proud name, *Gettysburg*.

"Wish we had her speed" grumbled the Captain.

He had been tense and gruff to his officers of late. Poor man, he had a lot to be worried about. Until America entered the war, no U–boats operated West of 40 degrees West Longitude. But we had heard some disturbing things on the American Radio, which has never been short on sensationalism. According to Texas Radio, ships were being torpedoed right on the Atlantic Seaboard. It was a long way to New York without the protection of convoy. Some years later a ship laden with ammonium nitrate was to decimate the town, but, even in 1941 it was a pleasant little port. We got busy – loading 87. octane.

Once the *San Amado* passed Key West, her speed gradually built up till she was doing fifteen knots. This was, of course, due to the Gulf Stream, which flows northward up the Florida Coast.

Now the Captain opened his Secret Orders, to find that he was instructed to proceed in daylight hours only, going into some bay, creek or river to anchor for the night. A feeble attempt to avoid the attentions of U-boats now concentrating on the easy pickings to be found on the coast, as opposed to the harder nuts of the British convoys.

Once we had passed Jacksonville, evidence of this was all too visible. The Atlantic coast line of the States has a broad, fairly shallow continental shelf, across which the sea channels are marked by large whistle buoys. The U-boats soon found out that it was childishly easy to pick off ships. All they had to do was to hang around within earshot of a whistle buoy, whose powerful, mournful note could be heard for several miles. Sooner or later a ship would come along and "Blam"! another tanker (oh, yes, most of the traffic was tankers), would go up. If the U-boat was unsuccessful at the whistle buoys, he had another alternative. The Americans, through carelessness or sheer blind folly, had no blackout of the coastal towns. Oh, sure, from time to time they had a "Brown Out", as a token gesture. But American cities were so well lit, that there was still a considerable background of light. From the low hull of a submarine passing ships were silhouetted against the loom of city lights. It must have been like taking toffee from a child. The ravages of shipping by U-boats on the Eastern Coast of America during January and February 1942 were immense. In one morning watch, from eight to noon, I counted sixteen ships in sight, all of which had been sunk, shelled, or were burning or sinking. One that we passed at breakfast time, quite close, was *Gettysburg*, abandoned, her bows riddled with shell holes, a huge column of oily, black smoke pouring from her torn tanks.

I mentioned shelling. U-boats were having such a free hand that, rather than use valuable torpedoes, they would surface and use gunfire to set a tanker on fire. The Americans had mounted dummy wooden guns on the poops of some of their tankers, but the Germans were not fooled for an instant. One Yankee ship was actually pursued by a submarine, firing its machine gun.

My recollection of this trip was firstly the mournful "Hoo, Hoo" of a whistle buoy as we steamed past it on a steel grey evening, waiting for the impact of a torpedo; and secondly the rattle and splash of the anchor cable in numberless bays and inlets. The Mate insisted that the senior apprentice should always be on the focsle head with him, when anchoring, which is why I am an expert in the anchoring of ships today.

And on the skyline, the blimps, the only real deterrent to the submarines. Small airships, filled with helium and propelled by two aero engines, they were capable of sixty miles an hour and could drop depth charges. Personally, I think the Germans gave the blimps credit for being more dangerous than they actually were. Certainly, when the silver cigar shape of a blimp nosed along the horizon, there was little evidence of U-boats.

At last San Amado reached Cape Hatteras. It is off this bleak sandspit, that the weather changes from the warmth of the Tropics to the cold of the temperate zone. Within the space of four hours the air and sea temperature will fall drastically.

I went on watch at noon in whites. By four o'clock I had to go below and change into "Blues". Some change in temperature.

Two days later, the pilot boarded us off the Ambrose Lightship, the landfall for the port of New York. When he heard where we had come from, he whistled under his breath.

"You're the first ship to arrive from Texas for the past week. All the others have been sunk".

We could believe him.

For the first time I saw the fabulous skyline of New York. Manhattan Island, as we came to an anchorage in the Upper Bay, was a thing of incredible beauty to our blackout-conditioned eyes. Tall pillars of a thousand lights, reaching up into the clouds. The flash of car headlights, the crimson and emerald glow of countless neon signs, dazzled our eyes, and numbed our senses. I was on watch in the morning as daylight came. Manhattan was hidden in mist. Then, as the light grew stronger, the tall spires of the skyscrapers began to pierce the mist, now rapidly dissolving in wreathes and spirals between the dark canyons of the buildings. All at once the sun broke from behind a cloud, and there, in all its splendour of steel framed concrete and glass walled castellations, was the Battery.

We had on board two young U.S.Coastguardsmen. Fresh out of training school, they hardly knew bow from stern. I am afraid we rather kidded them. One song, to the tune of the U.S. Marines "Halls of Montezuma" could be guaranteed to annoy, and scarcely help the cause of Anglo-American friendship. It went like this.

"From the shores of Coney Island to the Statue of Liberty,
We will fight our country's battles on the land or on the sea.
With a bottle of Pepsi-Cola, and a carton of ice cream,
We are bloody good lads in harbour, but – Oh, my God – at
sea!"

In order to avoid the U-boats as much as possible, *San Amado* was routed inside Long Island, and through the Cape Cod Canal. She moved through the jumble of ferries, tugs and lighters, from the Hudson into the East River. Behind on Bedloe's Island (in Upper New York Bay), the Statue of Liberty pointed her torch into the sky. As we sailed under the Brooklyn Bridge it seemed as if our masts must touch the roadway, though there was a hundred feet or so clearance. We passed the slums of Harlem, the piers and wharves of the East side, and soon were sailing past the yacht basins and mansions of Long Island. Names like Flatbush, Flushing, Port Washington, finally Martha's Vineyard and the Canal itself, cutting across the Cape Cod Peninsula. There are no locks on this waterway, and the scenery was lovely. Wonderful Colonial houses, whose gardens ran right down on to the canal bank, their occupants waving a welcome and farewell to *San Amado*. By evening on the second day out from New York she cleared the canal and steamed out across the Bay of Fundy, en route for Halifax. Some of the Cape Cod houses had "widow's walks" white painted verandas which ran along the seaward side of the bedrooms, from which, in a previous era, lonely wives could watch for the return of their husband's ships.

As the ship approached Nova Scotia, down came the fog, a damp, ghostly shroud. It smelt really fishy, and one could imagine all sorts of sea creatures hiding in its pall. Mermaids, naiads, Neptune himself, playing about under cover of the fog.

The Messroom boy was a simple lad, so he was sent to the Chief Engineer for the "Key of the Fog Locker". The Chief sent him down to the engine room, and the Third Engineer told him to go to the Cook, who sent him back to the Mate.

He wandered round for about an hour, from one to the other, till he was once more in the engine room. This time the Third gave him a crank case spanner, weighting about twenty eight pounds. By this time the lad had caught on. He took the spanner to the Chief's cabin. The Chief was not at home, so he laid it neatly, all four feet of it, in his bunk.

Sable Island was passed in the late afternoon, a long low shape of bleak rock, shrouded in mist. In the early morning, the pilot boarded us from a dory, while the Pilot cutter, a Grand Banks schooner, lay off at a distance, and soon San Amado was letting go in the haven of Bedford Basin.

It was now midwinter, so cold that the launches running the liberty service to Halifax were continually encased in ice, like glass boats. One night it snowed, the next morning every ship in the anchorage had been transformed from mundane cargo carriers into crystalline ship models, sparkling under a pale sun, their hulls reflected in the dark water.

As soon as the convoy left Halifax it was enveloped in sea fog which was to last for eight days. How, one wonders, did a convoy of forty to fifty ships manage to form up into a convoy?

The answer is simple. Each ship towed a "Fog-buoy". This was a piece of four by four timber, about five feet long, painted white, with, at its forward end, an angled piece of flat board, roughly four feet by two. At the tail was fitted a simple metal scoop, designed to throw up a plume of water as the buoy was towed along. On the upper surface of the board was painted the ship's convoy number, usually in red. The fog-buoy was towed two cables astern, and a ship merely searched till she found the number of her next ahead. What, on the face of it, should have been chaos became, in a matter of hours, an orderly procession of ships. Here and there throughout the convoy, certain ships were designated "Sound and Signal Repeating ships". When the Commodore made a signal, either by sound, or on his "Christmas Tree" of red and green lights, these vessels repeated the order, and everyone was able to follow. Perhaps I have over simplified things, and made it sound too easy. But the system was sound, and though there were many narrow squeaks, and heart-stopping shocks for many a shipmaster, it was always rather wonderful after days of dense fog, to find the convoy intact – a bit straggly perhaps – but all there.

This time *San Amado* was diverted to Loch Ewe on the West Coast of Scotland "for orders". It was an eerie experience to steam down a Scottish sea loch, in the teeth of a blizzard, with only the fitful glimmer of the next ahead's blue stern light. All at once the sensation was that we were approaching a black wall. My impression was of something huge and immovable towering over us.

"Let go" The order rang out from the bridge, and "Chips" knocked off the brake of the windlass. Thankfully I listened to the roar and splash of the cable as we brought up.

At daylight the storm had cleared. We lay on a mirror-glass loch of wild and savage beauty. Three cables off, loomed a Scottish mountain.

Loch Ewe must have been one of the most isolated spots of the last war. Apart from the hamlet of Aultbea, the nearest civilised place was Inverness, reached only after a forty five mile journey in the bus to Achnasheen, then a forty mile train journey. Yet there were even a few Wrens stationed there.

A launch drew alongside. Over the rail came six soldiers, loaded with equipment, Lewis guns and boxes of ammunition. This was the first of the Maritime Anti-Aircraft Regiment, raised to provide gun crews for the Merchant Navy. They had horrific tales to tell of the East Coast and E-Boat alley, then undergoing a siege from Germany, using mines, E-boats and aircraft, in a determined effort to close British ports. The Captain returned from the Naval Control with our orders. We were bound for Shellhaven. If the Coast was as bad as we had been led to believe, what chance had *San Amado* of reaching London? Perhaps the luck which had been hers on the Yankee Coast would carry her through. One of the gadgets brought on board by the gunners, was a pile of bamboo and fine canvas. The Mate sent for me.

"Ever flown a kite, Son?"

"Yes, sir"

"Well, you and your mate get down on deck and sort that lot out. I want it flying this morning – from the masthead"

At some previous time the ship had been fitted with a sheave at her Mainmast head, with small deck leads to the pipe-line winch on deck. I had often wondered why they were there – now I would find out.

It was interesting work assembling the kite. When finished, it was a box-kite, roughly eight feet square. How were we to get it to the mast head? All I could see was piano wire leading to a drum extension on the barrel of the winch. I studied the instructions again. "The cod-line is for use in raising the kite to the mast head" Ah yes. Make fast here thus, and thus. In a few minutes all was ready.

I went to the winch and turned on the steam. My mate steadied the kite with one hand, with the other he held the cod-line. As soon as the piano wire tightened, the kite took off in a powerful, surging swoop. There was a wail from Eric, and I looked up from the winch to see his boot soles soar over my head. Someone was yelling, "Let go! Let go!."

I stopped the winch and ran up on to the flying bridge. Eric had finally released his hold and was lying gasping and spluttering like a landed fish, while over our heads, the kite soared and swooped like a mad thing.

"You all right, Eric?"

"I think so. Gosh! I thought I was bound for Heaven that time!"

"Why didn't you let go?"

"I couldn't get my hand free. I'd taken a round turn, you see, and it got foul round my arm"

The winch below us rattled out as the Bosun slacked away, and soon our kite was flying three hundred feet above us.

"What's the kite for?" asked someone.

"To stop aircraft – "

"Garn!"

Methil Roads in the Firth of Forth was full of shipping, when *San Amado* called to change convoys. The passage round from Loch Ewe, through the Pentland Firth, had been uneventful, leaving the pessimists on board to remark gloomily,

"Don't you fret, Jerry's bound to get us before we get to London"

On board *San Amado* we felt very much the big ship, beside all the tiddlers, though we were to find out that the small ships knew the coast like the back of their hands. Leaving Methil, all the convoy had as escort was an old destroyer and an armed trawler. The N.C.S.O., the Naval Control Service Officer, had dumped a packet of coastal chartlets on board. These were sections of chart about 8" x 10" , with the convoy routes printed in red ink on their surface.

"Cor, Second Mate, Just take a look at that lot!"

By fitting three or four together, rather in the fashion of a jig-saw puzzle, we got about six hours steaming laid out on the chart table. Those little chartlets were invaluable, for they saved much time in laying off and plotting courses.

Once the convoy passed Flamborough Head, down came the fog. Cold, penetrating, beading steelwork and rigging with tiny droplets of moisture. By the time the convoy had reached the Sheringham Buoy, off the Norfolk Coast, darkness had closed in. The Sheringham was the recognised entrance to E-Boat Alley. Would we encounter any tonight?

The fog thickened, and soon the convoy had to anchor. Ships were not allowed to give the normal signal for a ship at anchor, that of ringing the ship's bell. All round was silence and fog. Orders were to create as little noise as possible, for the E-boats favourite method was to stalk a convoy under cover of fog, their powerful engines a mere whisper of sound, as they listened for the sounds which would betray a ship. The clank of an anchor chain – the slam of a door – even the whistle of a seaman walking along the deck, was enough to give away a vessel. Then the blast of a torpedo, and the shattering roar of Mercedes engines as the E-boat raced off into the impenetrable darkness.

A gunner phoned from his station on the poop.

"A launch has just gone past, sir, quite slowly"

It must have been an E-boat. We waited, as the minutes ticked away. Would he spot any ship? On this occasion, no. We heard no more of him.

Soon we reached the Sunk Pilot Station, still in the East Coast haze, where we picked up our pilot for London River. He came on board, wearing his life-jacket.

"Surely it's not as bad as that, Pilot?"

"Aye" said the pilot grimly, "I've been mined three times in the last month. They've got a new kind. Acoustic – goes off when it hears your engines."

Within five minutes, there wasn't a man on board not wearing a life jacket. *San Amado* reached Shellhaven without incident and got rid of her cargo safely.

This time in port, we had news of the *San Cipriano* being bombed on her way to Murmansk, of the *San Calisto* being mined in the Humber, of the *San Demetrio* in the Jervis Bay convoy, the *San Gerardo* was missing off Halifax, as was the *San Florentino* somewhere at sea. The *San Felix* had also been bumped but had made it to St. John, New Brunswick. It seemed as if half the fleet was being destroyed and, if this was happening to our Company, how then, was the rest of the Merchant Navy affected? The newspapers and radio only published the tonnage sunk, not the names of the ships, and often the tonnage figures were given in "Net Tons" – the smallest tonnage figure. Even they were rising.

I paid a visit to London with some of the other chaps. We were looking for some fun, to get a break from war, but in "the smoke" in 1942 the evenings seemed to be spent going from one shelter to another. Finally in disgust we managed to get a taxi, to take us to a little club, where tired men and women tried to give the impression of gaiety. Maybe it was we who could not but contrast life in the States with life in wartime Britain but we were glad to sail next day, out through the Barrow Deep, past the new Anti-Aircraft towers, to drop the pilot and proceed in convoy to Methil. This time, I made a flying visit to my home, only a few miles from Methil.

When I got back to Methil next afternoon, it was blowing a Northeast gale. I went in search of the N.C.S.O's drifter.

"Dinna worry, laddie. The convoy'll no be sailin' the nicht"

But I was not so sure. I didn't want to miss my ship. At dusk, the drifter skipper decided to go off. He had heard the convoy was sailing. I sat down in the tiny cabin, with some fellows from other ships. It smelt powerfully of fish and bilge water. Once the little fishing boat left the shelter of the harbour wall she met the full fury of the sea. She dived and swooped alarmingly. I looked at my companions. In the greenish glare of the gas light their faces looked ghastly. I hoped mine did not show how I was feeling.

A shout from the wheelhouse brought us up on deck. We were alongside *Amado*, but what was happening? She was under way.

"This is your ship, laddie?" the skipper shouted to me above the roar of the wind.

"Yes"

"Well. Stand by up here. When I say "Jump" – jump like hell"

The two vessels were bumping and grinding together. One minute the deck of the drifter was level with the tankers, and next it would be fifteen feet below, while a big sea foamed over the bulwarks. If I missed my jump, it was curtains, that was for sure.

The drifter rose on a wave, higher, higher, a voice bellowed in my ear.

"Noo, laddie, Jump"

I jumped, and landed sprawling clean over the rails of the *Amado*. I looked round to yell my thanks to the skipper, but the drifter was already fifty feet astern, falling away into the early Spring gloom.

It was a lousy trip round the coast to Loch Ewe. At one time we only covered seventeen miles in a watch. The Atlantic is rough, but the North Sea, in an ugly mood, can be just as bad.

After an uneventful outward convoy, it was once again Curacao for us. We loaded part cargo, then went to Aruba, for completion for an unknown port.

Aruba had been shelled not long before, by a U-boat. I saw a man in the San Nicholaas Club proudly display part of a shell, which had struck his house. Curiously enough, it was made of what looked like granite.

From Aruba we sailed for Port of Spain, Trinidad. This is one of the most beautiful islands of the West Indies. It has pleasant towns, wonderful beaches, and above all, towering in azure grandeur, the mountains.

The first ship we saw after entering the Boca del Dragone was *San Gaspar*. There had been rumours of her being torpedoed off Tobago with severe loss of life. We sailed past in silence. Now for the first time I got a close up view of the damage a torpedo could inflict. Under her bridge there was a great jagged hole, nearly a

hundred feet across. Fire and suffocation had been the main cause
of the casualties. Her bridge was a ruin, a blackened, twisted mass
of tangled metal. From a set of davits, a lifeboat, miraculously
untouched by the fire, hung, forlorn, from one set of blocks.

The Trinidad pilot said softly,

"They found seventeen bodies in the port midships alleyway"

We sailed independently next day still in the dark as to our
destination. The buzz was West Africa but we could not be sure. After
several days on a South Easterly course, we passed the islands of
Fernando Noronha, lonely fingers of black rock, pointing to the sky.

The method of sailing independently was this. The Captain was
given Route Instructions, with positions, through which the ship
had to pass, and secret Recognition Signals to be displayed should
a strange ship or aircraft challenge us.

The Mate decided that as he did not know when he would be
able to replenish his fresh water tanks, he would ration the drinking
and domestic water. We bathed in a bucket of sea water, in which
we also washed our clothes. Bars of "Sea-water soap" were issued,
but the results of our laundry efforts was not satisfactory, and there
was a spate of "Dhobi-Itch" among the crew. Most uncomfortable
with everyone walking straddle-legged! Oh, for a packet of modern
detergent.

One dark night, I was on the first watch with the Third Mate. It
was raining, a fine misty drizzle, which affected the visibility more
than one would expect. The ship was about two days out of
Freetown, which we had learned was our destination.

"Something fine on the port bow sir" called the lookout from
his position on the focsle head. The Third Mate stared ahead then
yelled.

"Hard-a-Starboard"

He dashed into the wheelhouse to help the helmsman push
over the spokes.

I had the impression of a huge black mass hurtling past to port.
A gust of hot air and funnel fumes engulfed our bridge, and the
splash of a bow wave ran along *San Amado*'s hull. Then it was gone.
The Third Mate and I peered aft through our binoculars. I got a
glimpse of four tall funnels before the drizzle swallowed them up.

A bath in a bucket.

"My God" said the Third Mate "that was the *Aquitania*"

How near we had been to annihilation. At our combined speeds of well over thirty knots there would have been one hell of a bang.

Each day at eight bells, all hands mustered to be issued with quinine tablets, which they had to swallow before the eyes of an officer. This was accomplished with the aid of "Board of Trade" lime juice, and the fact of any refusal was noted in the log book. It was hard to say which tasted worse – the quinine or the lime juice. For this was no "Clear, green cordial" as portrayed in the T.V. Adverts. This was the stuff they issued to ships to prevent scurvy.

Highly concentrated, it was a dirty brownish yellow colour, with a powerful acid taste, which no amount of sugar could hide. From this issue of lime juice to the old sailing ship men evolved the term "Lime Juicer" or, more simply "Limeys" for British sailors.

One captain was so keen to avoid the dread disease that he placed a bucketful of the hated lime juice, into which he poured a bottle of gin, at the galley door and invited the men to help themselves. He never had a case of scurvy.

We anchored in Freetown, the capital of Sierra Leone, on a pouring wet afternoon. Soaring into the rain clouds above the town rose the Lion Mountains, from which the colony took its name.

We lay in the roadstead for fourteen days, and it never once stopped raining in that time. As the ship swung round her anchor in the hot humid air, everyone grew terribly depressed. The only diversion was the canoe boys, little fellows from five years up to manhood, who came off from the shore in frail canoes, and dived for pennies.

"Massa, Massa Dash me penny. Dash me Liverpool Sixpence"

When a coin dropped into the dirty brown water, half a dozen lithe, brown bodies dived in. A flash of pink soled feet, beneath the coffee coloured water, then up would come a grinning boy, with the penny in his mouth, and nonchalantly swing into his canoe which had drifted on the tide at the same rate as the boy. How they never drowned I don't know, for the river was deep, and the current treacherous.

One fellow did not dive, but sang to an ancient ukulele "Show me the way to go home" with very naughty verses. Years later I was to pass through Freetown on my way to Ghana. That fellow was still singing his bawdy song.

On the tenth day in Freetown when we were beginning to despair of ever leaving the place, a naval launch appeared, with orders to put out fenders and prepare to tranship cargo to a Norwegian tanker called Petter.

There was much speculation as to the reason for this. The "Galley Wireless", that mysterious shipboard source of news, rumour, and plain old "Bull" offered three alternatives.

1. To be requisitioned as a Fleet oiler.
2. To be sent home for conversion to an aircraft carrier.
3. To be turned into a "Q" ship.

In the event all we did was transfer our complete cargo to the *Petter* and sail back to the West Indies.

This time *San Amado* loaded in a tiny port on the mainland of Venezuela. Called Puerto La Cruz. Never had we loaded cargo so fast.

In the 1940s the normal cargo loading of petroleum was 600/ 500 tons per hour. The young Cargo Supervisor said, matter-of-factly to the Mate

"'Kay. We'll just hook up four lines and let you have it at 3000 an hour!"

"3000?". Thinking in "Barrels", the Mate started to say "But that's only 75 tons – ". His voice trailed off. A look of incredulity spread over his fact.

"You mean – 3000 TONS per hour?"

"Yup! Tha's what Ah mean, Mr Mate".

So, with double banked watches, we loaded *San Amado* with twelve thousand tons of Venezuelan Crude in four hours.

Like the man said – we took it at 3000 tons an hour. So fast was this, that, by standing on the quay and watching carefully, it was possible to see the ship going down in the water. This was gravity loading. The tanks which fed our ship stood about half a mile away, but on top of a sixty foot cliff. From them to the loading manifold on the jetty, the oil was carried in 36 inch pipes, then from the manifold, through four eight-inch flexibles to our tanks.

No wonder *San Amado* sank visibly to her marks. Today such loading speeds are not uncommon, but the ships which take cargo at such speed are fine, modern tankers, built for the job, with large pipeline systems. We had only steel measuring tapes and "Ullage Sticks", graduated wood sticks about six feet long, to do a quick "dip" of the tank as the oil neared the top. When oil is flowing into a tank at speed, only a few feet below the deck, and all one has is a six-inch sight hole through which to push the dip-stick, in order to bring the oil to within a foot of so of the top, it requires quick wits and presence of mind. Only once in all my time on tankers did I witness an overflow, and that was due to a faulty pipeline, rather than human error. It was a spectacular jet of naphtha, sixty feet high.

In Puerto La Cruz, I again came up against the problems of drunken crews. The Merchant Seaman of to-day is a pretty reasonable fellow. Perhaps not so professional a seaman as he was a generation ago. He comes to sea for a few years, to see the world, till his girl prevails on him to chuck it and get a shore job. This is the main reason for the large turnover of men in the Merchant Navy. Before the 1939/1945 war, the Merchant Seaman conformed largely to the description which had fitted the sailor for years. "Every finger a marline-spike, every hair a rope-yarn and blood of Stockholm Tar". He had sailed on all kinds of ships, all over the world. His whole life was the sea.

If he had a wife and family, they were merely someone to whom he sent his allotment each month, names to put in the space in the Articles for "Next-of-kin". Someone to visit on his rare leaves. So Jack tended to live for the moment. Philosophically he would accept a long trip on a hard ship, knowing that he must pay off sometime, hoping that in some port he would find a better time. An incurable optimist.

Now, in Puerto La Cruz, our crew had discovered that a good time was to be had very cheaply. The town consisted of one street, and every house and bar was wide open. At sailing time there was no sign of the crew. After blowing the whistle several times, the Captain said

"Righto, Third Mate. Take two lads and fetch those heroes back aboard".

We set off up the hot, dusty road. We were tired and thought it a bit much to have to spend our break before sailing, searching for a crowd of drunks. The Third was an old hand at this game, having done it many times while on the run to Mexico.

"Now, Lads", he said, "You stay in the street and when I get them out, head them back to the ship".

He disappeared into the first bar, a dilapidated frame shack, from which came the sounds of merriment. In a few minutes, he reappeared with three or four sailors, drunk as lords. Behind, came several women, protesting vigorously in Spanish.

We progressed up the street. Once the sailors got out into the fresh air, they realised it was time to go home. Most of them came, meekly enough. All but one fireman. As fast as he was hauled out of one shack, he dived straight back into another. Eventually, rolling, staggering, they were herded back to the wharf. I felt like a sheepdog.

In the afternoon, we lay a mile off shore, awaiting our escort, a U.S. Patrol Boat. We went for a row in the jolly boat. The San Amado had no Shetland boat, so we had to make do with what was available. The jolly boat was only twelve feet long and was normally used for painting round the ship, so she was a far cry from the sweet and lovely dinghies I had been used to. Still, she was a boat, and we set off amongst the group of rocky islets to the West of the port. The water was like green crystal. We could look right to the bottom, a wonderland of living, coloured coral. A myriad of fishes of all shapes and colours, darted and hovered as they fed on the reef. It was one of the most wonderful afternoons I had yet spent at sea. Swimming, diving from rocks or lazing in the sun on a tiny beach, composed of coral particles. This was the life.

San Amado made three trips to and from Puerto La Cruz and Aruba, before anchoring in Oranjestad Harbour to clean tanks. After carrying Venezuelan Crude, this was a ghastly job, as not only was the residue black and oily, it was extremely gassy. It took over a week, working night and day, to get the San Amado's tanks fit to load spirit cargoes once again. The Bosun was put in charge of one tank cleaning gang, and I, as Senior Apprentice, in charge of the other.

Each compartment was steamed with caustic soda. A steel drum of this chemical was punched full of holes. Fitted into its top was a one inch copper steam hose. The whole contraption was lowered into the tank to be cleaned, and the caustic steam allowed to play over the steel surfaces for four hours. The tank lid was then lifted and a man with a hot water hose went down into the tank and washed it down, the pump sucking the drainings away, the while.

Sleeping in the tropics – too hot below.

It was a hellish task. The caustic steam stung one's eyes and raised blisters on exposed skin. We wrapped burlap round our hands and wore oilskins and seaboots. The temperature in the tank was around a hundred and fifty, it was murder. I lost some weight that week! So fed up were we at the end of the job, that the Bosun and I went ashore to look for a job on the West Indies schooners. We got the offer of berths on a salt schooner, but at the last moment got cold feet. We weren't too sure if being shot was the penalty for deserting the Merchant Navy in time of war.

At last the job was done, but instead of loading in the West Indies, the ship left for Port Arthur, Texas, to load the new 100 Octane petrol. Rumour had it that the only place where this high power juice was used was in the Russian Front. For us, that meant only one port – Murmansk. Any way, we again sailed up the Atlantic Seaboard of America, this time protected by PT boats, blimps, Coastguard and Converted Ice Patrol cutters. We saw nothing of the Germans, and once more it was Halifax for convoy and the long haul across the "Western" for home.

Arrived in the Clyde the ship was ordered to anchor well up Loch Long, "Where the Russian ships muster for convoy" according to the indefatigable "Galley Wireless". Still, there must have been something in it, for our fate hung in the balance for two days. Then we were sent South to the Mersey for discharge.

I had been eight months on *San Amado* and was sent home on leave.

4

WINTER – NORTH ATLANTIC

It was late Autumn, 1942. Being out of England for such long periods, enabled one to see the effects of the war and shortages on the people of Britain. In London and other big cities, people were living like troglodytes, surfacing only to go to work each day. Nights were spent in shelters of one kind or another, from an Underground station to an Anderson in the back garden. In contrast to the States, the population looked shabby. Here were no well dressed, nylon stockinged girls, though the legs, in lisle threads, might be just as attractive. Everything was on points, coupons, or rationed in some way. Restrictions were the order of the day. Going into a shop, to buy something, only to be told,

"Sorry, none to be had. Don't you know there's a war on?"

That being exactly what I did know, there was no suitable answer. I began to long to return to sea. There was freedom. In spite of the ruthlessness of the German Kriegmarine, in spite of the awful death in a blazing tanker; for a young man, there was a spice to life, a feeling that it would never happen to you. There were the good moments, which, in retrospect, always outshone the bad. I fretted, in spite of the comfort of being at home. Shore life was so terribly narrow.

At last the telegram came, from Mr Eagle. I was to join a brand new ship, then completing in the Furness Shipbuilding Company's yard at Haverton Hill-on-Tees. I arrived in Middlesbrough. Once again it was November and raining. After arranging with the ship's agents about accommodation in the town, I crossed the Tees on (or should it be in?) the Transporter Bridge, to Port Clarence, where I got a bus up the road to the shipyard. Through the big gates, to the Office. In the yard were several ships, one of which caught my eye. She was surely the ugliest vessel ever built. Thank goodness

Eagle had good ships, that I would not have to sail on a tub like that.

At the office a pleasant faced yard manager offered to show me the way to *Empire Cobbett*.

"She's not far away. Go round the end of the big shed and that's her, lying in the basin".

I followed his instructions and to my horror, the ship which loomed in the basin, was the ugly duckling. Some 15,000 tons dead-weight, nearly 500 feet long, she was the ugliest ship I was ever to sail on. Amidships, an untidy heap of accommodation repeated itself on the poop, out of which latter rose a thin woodbine of a funnel. To further disfigure her ungainly appearance she was fitted with three "Goal-post masts", one forward, one amidships, and one aft behind the funnel. Painted overall a uniform grey, she was far removed from the sleek motorship I had had in mind.

Once again I was Senior Apprentice, which I had long since found to be a doubtful honour. All it meant was that any job too distasteful for the crew, was given to the boys. Things like cementing the inside of the fresh water tanks, cleaning bilges, doing any extra duty watches there might chance to be; and withal, learning to be a ship's officer.

I did learn a lot in those early years. The satisfaction of a smartly dressed message, the sweet coil of a heaving line, as I threw it right at the feet of a dock hand. The handling of a back spring wire, knowing just the precise moment to slack it before it snapped.

Master of *Empire Cobbett* was Captain Dudley Mason GC It was his first ship after his epic voyage in the *Ohio* to Malta. I was thrilled to be sailing under such a man. He proved, as all real heroes are, to be a very modest man, and an excellent shipmaster.

Outward bound we got a terrible pasting from the weather. After running trials off Newbiggin, Northumberland, we rounded the North of Scotland to go into Loch Ewe and join the Atlantic convoy. The new apprentice had to be left in Loch Ewe. Somehow in the few days he had been on board, he had contracted pneumonia. I kept finding him asleep in the most unlikely places, at the most inconvenient moments. When the doctor had come out from Aultbea to inform the captain that the boy had pneumonia we were very surprised at the diagnosis. Still the Doc could not be wrong.

Now we were at sea, in a howling wilderness of storm and blizzard, which screamed endlessly down on the convoy, out of the North-west. Great blasts of Arctic Air, snow-burdened, and blinding, smothered the convoy. Now there was no need to look out for the enemy. He was here but he was not a German submarine. He was – Cold. The kind of cold which numbs not only a man's flesh, but, through the resultant slowing down of the circulation, also slows his brain. In extreme cases, this could result in a man, standing on watch, freezing to death, almost before anyone realised it. Ships grew sluggish, under the ever increasing burden of ice and snow. The sea itself, as it hit the steel decks, froze into a slushy porridgy mush, which soon hardened to solid ice. Though this was not particularly dangerous to a tanker, with her great margin of stability, it could prove fatal to a smaller ship, such as a destroyer or corvette. That none of them were lost was due to the superhuman efforts of their crews, who must have spent countless hours, chipping ice from the superstructure; in sub zero temperatures, absolute agony to tired and exhausted men. And the *Empire Cobbett* rolled. God! how she rolled. She had the worst motion of any ship I was ever on. In her ballast condition she whipped in a fore and aft direction. This is not unusual for tankers, but *Empire Cobbett* far surpassed any normal ship. For want of better we called the movement "Bucking". To stand on the poop, by the taffrail, was impossible for any length of time, for the bucking made one dizzy and light-headed. It was also scarifying to watch 490 odd feet of ship undulating across the Atlantic, as if emulating a sea-serpent.

Running along a bucking deck has two sensations. That of weightlessness as the deck drops from under one's feet, and of weighing far more than normal as it changes and rises rapidly beneath one. The first makes a man run on tip toe, and the second causes his knees to buckle.

In each case he has not full control of himself for a rolling movement of the ship may complicate the equation of balance.

The goal post masts were to be fitted at a later date with "Admiralty Net Defence", a system of anti-torpedo nets hanging

In a howling wilderness of storm and blizzard.

Under the ever increasing burden of ice and snow. (*Courtesy of J. B. Nash*)

along each side of the ship, like a pair of lace curtains. The winches for the operation of the nets had already been built into the ship. In all there were fourteen winches to be kept from freezing, during this ghastly voyage. Who by? Of course, the Apprentices. I was the only apprentice, so the job fell to me. Going round regularly to oil and see that each winch was ticking over, and that the pistons did not freeze up. So cold was it that at each winch I had to stick the oil can under the steam drains, open them for several minutes so that the live steam could warm the oil sufficiently to make it flow. The task was like painting the Forth Bridge. No sooner had I finished aft than it was time to start forward again.

After ten days of this hell, we broke from the convoy and headed south west for warmer weather, bound for Texas.

My sojourn aboard *Empire Cobbett* was uneventful. She was a ship I never liked. At sea she rolled all the time, like a spud in a pot. Loaded she was more like a submarine than a ship. Perhaps that's why she was never torpedoed. Any sub spotting her as she dived through a sea, would be bound to turn away, thinking "It's one of ours". We used to submerge off Cape Hatteras and surface off Malin Head.

Empire Cobbett eventually got her A.N.D. nets. She went to Barrow-in-Furness to have the booms fitted. While there I saw one of the famous X-craft, being lowered into the water by a crane. These were to do sterling work attacking the *Tirpitz* as she lay in Alta Fjord.

From Barrow, we went round to the Albert Basin, Bidston, in the Mersey, where the actual nets and running gear were fitted by a gorgeous bunch of swell little Wrens, who not only carried out their work most efficiently, but also carried off the ship's entire sweet ration for the voyage, AND the saloon clock from its place on the bulkhead.

Trials of the new gear were made in Liverpool Bay, as the ship steamed up and down between the Bar and North-west Lightships. The winch operators and the Chief Mate, were connected to each other by a telephone inter-com system. I learned more fancy cuss-words in the next half hour than I had known existed until then.

"Out Booms" The hundred foot booms swung overboard from their stowed positions to an angle of forty-five degrees. Then, "Draw

Nets" With a sibilant, swishing sound, the steel meshed nets ran smoothly forward and aft from their stowed positions on the Midships pair of booms.

"Lower to Ninety" Here was where the fun began. As the forward booms got the weight of the nets entering the water, and the drogue took up the slack, it was impossible for the winches to hold the strain. Even putting them in gear, without steam, was not enough to hold the booms. So the forward pair of booms dropped quickly to the horizontal, to be followed more leisurely by the Midships, and finally the after pairs of booms. The handbook said they should all go up and down in unison, but maybe the boffin who dreamed that one up, had never tried a practical demonstration. Anyway, there we were, festooned with nets on either side, like a ruddy fishing boat. Our full speed of 11.5 knots was reduced by two knots by the drag of the nets.

Though we sneered at the A.N.D. system we did get an opportunity of seeing that to some extent it was effective. As we returned to the anchorage, we passed a cargo boat fitted with A.N.D. which had just come in. Her starboard net hung at forty-five degrees. Entangled in its folds were the sinister, cigar shapes of two torpedoes.

In September 1943 I left *Empire Cobbett* to go up for my Second mate's ticket. I had two month's leave, and was allowed an extra month's paid leave by the company to attend nautical school.

Leith Nautical College was founded in about 1860s. It stands well along Commercial Street, across the Water of Leith. Thousands of M.N. officers have passed through it. At the time I attended, the Principal was Mr. Fisher, a small dapper man, with a wonderful fund of nautical knowledge, and a more wonderful manner of imparting it to seamen who might be as "Thick as two short planks". His staff of instructors, men who had been in command of a ship, were excellent. Not only did they know their stuff, they also knew how to handle young and flighty officers, firmly but encouragingly.

We did a lot of hard work in our three months at school, as we plodded through navigation chartwork, ship construction, meteorology, seamanship and the other hundred and one things in the curriculum.

Seamanship was held every morning for an hour by Captain Mowat. He was a "Teuchter", a highlandman, with the soft sibilant speech of his kind.

"Chust tell me, Mr. Steefenson, what iss a spirkatin' plate?" I finally discovered the whereabouts of this unlikely portion of a ship's anatomy, but never, during all my examinations, was I to be asked for it. By the time Captain Mowat had finished with us in the seamanship room, we knew the Rule of the Road (the International Regulations for Prevention of Collision at Sea) backwards, forwards and inside out, as well as the position of the splash plate.

At last the first day of the examinations. We trooped along to the Board of Trade Examination Rooms in Quality Street, to be greeted by the Examiner's Clerk. He ushered us into the waiting room, where there was much last minute perusing of notes and formulae, and several dashes to the toilet, just across the corridor. Came the summons, and we entered the examination room, a long high-ceilinged chamber, with tall windows all down one side. Each desk was well separated from its neighbour, to avoid any temptation to crib. Cheating was punishable by instant dis-qualification, but that did not deter the odd man from trying. From Monday till Friday the examinations ran. We attended each day, it seemed as if Friday would never come. On this day the last of the exams, the "Orals" were held, if one was well down the alphabet as I was.

On Saturday we attended the B.O.T. Rooms, anxious to get the results. I had passed. I was a fully fledged Second Mate. So was my pal. I turned to him.

"Congratulations – MISTER Ferguson" I pumped his hand.

"Congratulations – MISTER Stevenson"

We stared at each other then burst into laughter. We ran into the street, waving our buff slips.

"Now" I said firmly, "Let's go to the saddlers!"

"What for?" asked Fergy.

"For three years I've done nothing but answer two blasted whistles. Now I'm going to buy myself – a whistle"

We did. They cost us two and six. I still have mine, having used it as a ship's officer and Pilot for over twenty years.

I reported my success to Mr. Eagle and sat back to await the recall telegram.

* * *

San Vito slipped through the boom at five minutes past Midnight, on January 1st 1944. The log read "Wind South-west, force 6. Rain squalls, Poor Visibility" The Pilot tried to be jovial.

"Happy New Year everybody". The irony was not lost on me, a Scotsman, sailing from the Clyde on Hogmanay. I had joined San Vito on the eleventh December 1943, in Harland and Wolff's Govan Yard. My rank was Third Officer, and I was keenly aware of my new responsibility. So much had happened to me since I stepped on board San Conrado back in 1940. In experience of bridge work alone, I had gained immeasurably from convoy duty, far more than the average peace-time apprentice, who, apart from the times he cleaned the brass, usually stepped on to the bridge as a third officer completely ignorant of the finer points of running a watch. During my training in the convoys I had frequently been left in charge of the station-keeping, while the Officer of the watch did some work in the chart room, not far away. I would also attend to any signals that might be made. Though under the eye of a qualified officer, I gained confidence through the trust placed in me. I said that I got all the dirty jobs, and extra watches, while serving my time. This was true, but imperceptibly, the hard work, the little responsibilities, were building character, and qualities of seamanship, which, now that I had become an officer had fused into self reliance and confidence in my abilities.

San Vito was one of the Company's latest "V" Class ships. Some twelve thousand tons, she was fitted with Gyro-compass, which I thought was wonderful. She was also fitted with numberless guns. They poked out at one from every corner. There was a 4.7 Dual purpose on the poop, as well as a twelve-pounder AA gun. There was a gunpit on the bows, though no gun had yet been fitted. Technically, by International Law, this would have made us a "Warship" as merchant ships were supposed only to have guns mounted aft, to fight while running away. To complete the armament, there were eight 20mm. Oerlikon Cannon, as well as

P.A.C. rockets, and a Hydrogen filled balloon barrage. Things had progressed somewhat from the days of Box-kites.

San Vito ran her trials during the short winter afternoon of 31st December 1943. From somewhere high up in the organisation of Harland and Wolff's the order had been given that the ship had to be handed over to her owners before the end of the year. The reason for this was obvious, of course – twelve thousand extra tons of shipping built in 1943. What it meant in terms of human worry and endeavour was much more than the bald figures indicated. The sweat of scores of shipyard fitters in the engine, room, the sheer hard graft of those on deck, doing the last minute jobs. The efforts of San Vito's crew, taking stores, and desperately trying to prepare the ship for sea.

As San Vito turned for her last run over the measured mile, it was four thirty, and already dark. The odds against her being handed over that year seemed impossible. The engine was giving a little trouble, the lifeboats were not even stored, and the last of the stores had not yet come aboard.

At six-thirty p.m. Captain Smith and Mr. Welch, the Engineer Superintendent for Eagle, signed the papers, accepting San Vito from Harland and Wolff, for Eagle Oil and Shipping Company. All the dockyard mateys swarmed off the ship into the waiting launch, and she moved slowly to an anchorage at the Tail o' the Bank. The Master had already been to the Convoy Conference, earlier in the day, and San Vito was "In all respects ready for sea."

We sailed for New York. The last time I sailed from the Clyde had been as a first tripper, on a beautiful summer evening. Now I was again sailing from the Clyde, on my first trip as Third Officer. Only, this time, it was mid-winter.

On Saturday, 1st January 1944 the convoy had formed, in poor visibility, and a moderate gale. At three thirty on Sunday afternoon, we were given a new position, Number 93, third ship in the starboard outside column. Ahead of us was a tanker belonging to C.T. Bowring, the El Elito. Her master was Captain Smith's brother.

By this period in the Battle of the Atlantic, the Royal Navy was beginning to get a stranglehold on the U-boats.

I noticed the difference at once. The convoy was much better disciplined. Overhead, Coastal Command planes patrolled to their limits, and the "Gap" was covered by the convoy's own aircraft carrier, the M.A.C. ship (Merchant Aircraft Carrier) from which flew Swordfish and Martlet planes. The Escort was good, three A/S frigates and four corvettes. In addition, special hunter/killer groups of A/S warships had been formed, to scour the Western Ocean, harrying and hunting the U-boats before they had a chance to form into a wolf-pack.

While I was on *San Amado* the only air cover over the "gap" between 30 and 60 degrees west was provided by the "CAM" ship, whose letters stood for "Catapult Aircraft Merchant Ship. This was an ordinary "Empire" cargo vessel, on whose bows, was fitted a special catapult ramp, from which a specially adapted Hurricane fighter could be shot off into the air, when occasion demanded. The occasion was provided by the Focke-Wulfe Condors of the Luftwaffe, who flew on reconnaissance, for the U-boats.

These long range aircraft would fly round and round a convoy, keeping just out of gun range, and relay the position of the convoy to the Nazi Naval H.Q. for transmission to the U-boats. They had a depressing effect on the crews of the merchant ships, for the lads knew that every move the convoy might make in the way of evasive action, would immediately be reported. Tales of merry signals where the S.O.E. signalled to a Condor:-

"Please fly round the other way – you are making us dizzy" and the plane complying, were drawing the long bow a bit. Be that as it may, no merchant seaman had a good word for the Condors.

In 1936 the Kreigsmarine wanted a long range aircraft capable of making armed reconaissance sorties in co-operation with U-boats far out into the Atlantic Ocean. But under Hitler, German Military strategy was based on "blitzkrieg" using short and medium range dive and horizontal bombers. Large warships and naval air craft were restricted as Hitler thought he could avoid a maritime war with Britain.

Admiral Doenitz continued to demand his long range bomber and he was fortunate that in 1939 Hauptmann Edgar Petersen had commanded a special school around 1936 to train flyers in long range flying, using flying boats and float planes. He thought it might be possible to convert the four engined Focke Wolfe 200 Condor passenger transport for armed reconaissance over the sea.

The Germans re-designed the plane for fuel range, bombs and guns reckoning the radius of action could be 931.5 miles and duration 15 hours. The crews were five men. Pilot, co-pilot, navigator, engineer and rear gunner.

So successful was this aircraft that had the Germans only realised it, they could have sunk more allied shipping by this means than by the vastly more expensive U-boats in terms of materials and manpower. Very fortunately for us, they did not. In total 262 Condors came off the production line but the increase in air defences of convoys using CAM ships, MAC ships, escort carriers and more heavily armed anti-air craft merchant ships, all meant that the Condor never really succeeded except with one successful attack on our 42,500 ton *Empress of Britain*, setting her on fire and sinking. They were based at KG40 (Kampfgeschwader) bomber group between Bordeaux and Merignac.

What greatly helped the defeat of "Condor" was that Dr Salagar of Portugal allowed Britain to use Tercira in the Azores for Squadrons 206, 220 and 223.

However, as soon as the CAM ships made their appearance the situation was reversed. Now it was the Condor who was the worried man. Out of the blue, retribution was apt to strike. Only once did I witness a CAM ship in action, and it was a masterly and memorable performance.

One wet and dismal afternoon, a Condor was heard above the cloud base. There could be no mistaking that unsynchronised beat of the engines. Then he appeared through a gap in the cloud. We cursed him unavailingly, for we knew that the convoy's position would soon be in the hands of the nearest U-boats.

There was the roar of a plane from the far side of the convoy. The bows of the CAM ship disappeared in a cloud of steam, as the powerful catapult went into operation. Like an arrow the vengeful outline of the Hurricane climbed into the sky. Meanwhile, the Condor, sensing trouble, had dodged back into the clouds. We listened with all our ears. Came the zoom of aircraft in fierce manoeuvring, the chatter of guns, then out of the scud came the fighter, doing victory rolls all over the sky. Of the Condor there was no more sign.

The Hurricane flew around for about an hour "Beating up" the convoy. Then he climbed steeply into the clouds. Minutes later the plane reappeared in a power dive, straight into the sea. What had happened? Not for long were we left in doubt. Out of the sky floated a parachute. Below, a waiting destroyer was no further than 80 yards away. Down went her sea boat, and within minutes the gallant pilot had been picked up.

Not all such pilots were so lucky. Many were killed, as surely as if they were shot, by the freezing sea and wind, before rescue could be made. Some were drowned, dragged down by their heavy clothing and a waterlogged parachute. Some, alas, were never seen again, due to the appalling weather. All honour to these brave airmen who, suicidal though it was, attempted the protection of men they had never seen.

Anyhow, on this voyage, apart from bad weather and fog, we had no excitement. On Tuesday, 18th January, San Vito queued for her pilot off the Ambrose Lightship, and headed up the swept channel into New York Upper bay. In the early afternoon she berthed at No. 1 Pier, Hoboken. Dockyard men from Todd Shipbuilding boarded to do some engine repairs, for the engine had not been entirely to the Chief's liking all the way across. There was also a rumour that we were to carry planes, though no one took much notice of such a preposterous idea. Where could we carry planes? On Sunday, after the engine repairs were finished, San Vito left Hoboken and moved up river on the Manhattan side, to berth at Pier 90, North River, on the other side of a finger pier which held the Queen Mary. It was the first time I had seen her, and her huge yet graceful bulk was something to marvel at. It was surprising to find that most of the longshoremen thought she was an American vessel, built in the States.

No sooner were we tied up than four big scows came alongside. On each barge was a score of welding machines. What did they want?

"We're gonna give you a spar deck, so you can carry planes".

The buzz had been right. OK Let them put a spar deck on us. At least it would take some time, and time to we young fellows, meant shore leave.

The two senior boys and myself went ashore to marvel at New York. Broadway was wonderful. Times Square superb. We ended up in the British Merchant Navy Officers' Club on 44th Street. Here was every evidence of Anglo-American friendship. Everything was either free, or ridiculously cheap. We could get free tickets for shows, visits to radio stations, tours of the City. And the girls, "Waal, I guess they were jus' 'bout the mos' frien'ly in the world".

At Two o'clock in the morning, we found ourselves travelling the famous Long Island Railroad, with Ruth, Mary and Helen. Three sisters, daughters of a Presbyterian minister in Port Washington. They were utterly delightful companions, but thought we were crazy to travel thirty odd miles to see them home. Their parents could not have been kinder to us and each time we were in New York after that, we always called to "visit with them". Perhaps, in other and more circumstances, we might have married them, but alas, during our long voyage, which was to come, all three girls got married and no doubt lived happily ever after.

To our amazement, the spar deck was complete by breakfast next morning. How these Yanks hustled! It covered the main and fore decks "Like a perishing birdcage" as the Bosun succinctly put it. By noon, the longshoremen had started to load our deck cargo, five Mustang fighters, done up in cocoons and three giant packing cases each containing one complete troop glider.

San Vito moved from Pier 90, into the stream, to anchor. A few hours wait, then she went to the Socony Vacuum Terminal over in Bayonne, New Jersey, to load 100 Octane gasoline.

This did not take long, but it was not until 5th February, that she finally sailed in convoy. The delay had been due to waiting for a convoy to gather and to fog.

Once more, apart from fog and the usual bad weather, to which we were becoming inured, the trip was uneventful and sixteen days later we arrived in Barry Roads, preparatory to moving into Avonmouth. The planes were removed by an American team of airmen, and we moved outside to the Oil Berth, to discharge. By 3rd March we were feeling our way in a blizzard off Inistrahull, bound for New York.

After loading 100 Octane, we sailed for Lynnhaven Roads, to join a Mediterranean convoy. The galley wireless had the name of an Italian port, Bari.

During the night, a gale sprang up and most of the convoy dragged anchor. Some went on the beach. All except our ship. Her master was commended for his seamanship.

This convoy illustrated how Allied sea power had grown. Instead of forty odd ships, as in the old days of transatlantic convoys, there were ninety-six, mostly "Liberty". Included were some odd looking craft, which we soon discovered were L.S.Ts. The Liberty ships were as alike as peas in a pod. Where the U.S. was getting the men to man such vast merchant fleets we could only guess. We heard tales of young men in their twenties, after six months at school, being given command. How true was this? I don't know, but some of the antics the "Libertys" got up to made one wonder.

One story will illustrate what I mean. An American Liberty convoy arrived in Hvalfjord, Iceland.

"Get ready to anchor" said the Captain.

"Which anchor, Cap'n?" asked the Mate.

"How many we got?"

"Lemme see. There's two on the bow, one spare on the aft deck, and a small one".

"Put 'em all over!" said the Captain.

Whatever the Liberties lacked in seamanship, they made up for in armaments. The Americans had no qualms about International Law. Once it had been broken by the German Reich, they fixed guns all over the ships. On each Liberty ship's bow was a useful looking quick firing dual purpose gun, manned by naval ratings.

The escorts too, were more numerous than those of the purely British convoys. Here were sleek, deadly looking Destroyer Escorts, the ideal sub-chaser. Something of the order of fifteen escorts. We, on *San Vito* felt as safe as houses.

By the 9th April, the convoy had passed through the Straits of Gibraltar and had altered formation to two tremendously long columns, to pass through the minefields of the North African Coast. Two days later, we passed Algiers at dusk. The city was a blaze of light. It struck me as odd, that a town so near the theatre of war should be lit up. Perhaps it didn't matter much whether the city was illuminated or not – the German Air Force knew exactly where it was.

Algiers faded into a golden sunset and the convoy steamed on under a Mediterranean moon of breathtaking beauty.

Halfway through my watch, around ten, a plane was heard high in the starry sky. The Leading Gunner, on watch above me on Monkey Island, said lugubriously,

"I know that's a Jerry, Listen to his engine".

I listened. There was no mistaking that curiously unsynchronised beat. As we listened it faded off to the northwards.

"Gorn to tell 'is pal!" said our Job's comforter "E'll be back".

At eleven thirty, with half an hour of my watch left to go, all Hell was let loose. The German plane had been back with the convoy for some time, droning endlessly round the edges.

The Commodore ship erupted in a spectacular display of fireworks. As I pressed the tits of the Alarm Bells, I felt that familiar sinking thrill in the pit of my stomach. I was sure the Commodore had been attacked and bombed. By now the sky was full of tracer lines, green flares, the whole garishly illuminated by the brilliant splendour of star shells. A proper Brock's benefit.

On board I could hear the sound of running feet, doors slamming and loud and heart-felt curses, as someone stubbed his toe on a ladder rung.

SanVito had been issued with a Radio/telephone set called a TBS, in Lynnhaven for use in the Med. Now we switched it on. Fragments of conversation from escort to escort reached us.

"Jig One calling. Jig One calling. Now hear this. Now hear this – ".

Jig one was our Senior Officer Escort, a D.E. He was giving out some interesting information.

"18, One Eight aircraft bearing 360, three six zero degrees, approaching. There are also U-boats in the area".

Just about all we needed to complete the party.

Outside the wheelhouse, it was bedlam. All our guns were firing. So were those of every ship in the convoy. A veritable curtain of steel was being raised against the marauding bombers.

"Why so many green flares?" someone asked. The Captain answered

"The Germans have got a new bomb which they've been using on the Russian Convoys. It's a kind of glider bomb, launched from Heinkel IIIs and guided by a green light in the tail to its target. That's why the escort is firing green flares, to confuse the parent plane".

I went outside to stare through my binoculars at a steady green light approaching us. Sure enough, I cold make out what looked like a tiny plane − a winged bomb. Even as I watched, a spray of tracer shot up from a nearby D.E., and I ducked, as the bomb exploded in mid-air. I went back into the wheelhouse to my task of keeping station on the next ahead. It was safer.

The Captain and the Mate were listening intently to the TBS " − Fourteen aircraft. Two down − " Obviously we weren't doing so badly. Gradually the firing eased off. The planes had departed. Now, up the port side of the convoy raced a venerable British cruiser, I recognised as *Cleopatra*. She must have been doing close on thirty knots, belching out black and white smoke from her funnels, in the effort to hide the convoy from the eyes of the U-boats. Swiftly she crossed ahead of the convoy and ran down the starboard side. Moments later we entered a fog of oily smoke. When we cleared it the enemy had gone. It was one thirty.

The action had lasted three hours. To me it had been five minutes. Next day, on the TBS we heard a weak signal in German. Was this another plane that hadn't made it?

At 5.0 p.m. on Thursday 13th April , we sailed past the barren peninsula of Cap Bon. Through the glasses could be seen the wreckage of war, burnt out tanks, an up-ended field gun, wrecked trucks. It seemed incredible that the remnants of Rommel's famed Afrika Korps had so recently been crowded into that narrow neck of land by the victorious Eighth Army.

On a lovely Spring morning *SanVito* brought up in the anchorage of Port Augusta, having been piloted through the narrow entrance by a little Sicilian pilot, whose only English apart from the words "Royal Navy" on his battledress blouse, were, "Tutta Forza!" Since this meant "Full Speed" Captain Smith wisely ignored his advice and brought us in easy.

For the first time we saw what happens to a country when it is fought over by two great opposing armies. Desolation and destruction. Destruction, as sailors, we were used to. The total disintegration of a ship, when she is torpedoed. Incidentally, it is only in the trashier war books that one comes across the expression "Tinfished", when speaking of being torpedoed. I never heard a man, either Royal or Merchant Naval, use that flippant word. We all had too much respect for the destructive power of a torpedo, with its 500 pounds of Amatol in its warhead.

To return to Sicily. Round the bay, so beautiful in the brilliant sunshine, lay the wrecks of a score of J.U.52s. Those proud tripled engined troop carriers and bombers, which had struck such fear into the peoples of Europe. But it was the houses of the town that looked so pathetic, their white walls crumbled to dust, their shattered windows looking out on all the beauty of the bay, like the eyes of a sightless man.

In the distance the cone of Etna smouldered against a sky so blue that it hurt the eyes.

That night we were kept awake by a naval patrol going round dropping anti-personnel charges, to discourage enemy frogmen. It gave me a creepy feeling to think that even as I lay in my bunk, a frogman might be attaching a limpet mine to San Vitos's bottom.

Early in the morning, I watched a patrol go by, the naval skin divers who actually searched the bottoms of ships, if anything suspicious were reported, stood, shivering in the sternsheets. I did not envy them. The Dems ratings had been on watch all night, patrolling the decks, to listen for suspicious noises. We felt nearer the front line than at any time in the war.

In the late afternoon of the following day, Sunday 16th April, San Vito sailed as Commodore Ship of a small convoy of seven ships. Five were Libertys and the sixth was, like San Vito, an oil tanker. Her name was British Patience and she had come from the same yard, Harland's of Govan earlier in the year.

On board we had the Commodore, a tall red-faced N.O., who turned out to be a little peculiar. He had been too long in the Med., too long under fire. He was as nervous as a kitten. His staff of two signalmen and a leading signalman, were hard put to it to keep up with his incessant signals.

Expert as we were at convoy routine, that Commodore had us bamboozled by the amount of signalling. Flags flew from our triatic stay all day, hectoring, ordering this or that.

"Make less smoke."

"You are out of station" – followed by the number of the luckless ship.

"Alter course to so-and-so".

The Aldis lamps clicked endlessly, one from either bridge wing. After the peace and quiet of the Atlantic, where days would pass with little or no signalling, it was chaos. In any case, the Yankee ships paid little or no attention to his exhortations.

Slowly the little convoy crept round the heel of Italy into the Adriatic. Yet another signal flew from our halyard.

"Stream paravanes!"

What! Only the Navy did that!

Of course all merchant ships carried paravanes, but very few ever streamed them.

"Are you sure it's necessary, Commodore?" asked Captain Smith.

For answer the Commodore opened his brief case and invited the Captain to inspect the chart he took from it. I saw the Captain's face turn pale.

"Right Mr Mate, – get the paravanes over right away! We're on the edge of a minefield."

Some four hours and a lot of sweat later, I was able to look over the wing of the bridge, where the dim, porpoise like shape of the paravane swam some ten feet below the surface, at the end of its wire, which led from the boom slung over the bows. The idea of paravanes was that a mine mooring wire, coming into contact with the sweep wire of the paravanes, would slide down and outwards to the head of the paravane, where a serrated pair of steel jaws cut the mooring, enabling the mine to pop to the surface, where it was destroyed by gunfire.

The Adriatic Coast of Italy was unlit, save for a few lighthouses burning at reduced power. Our uneasiness at being so close to the minefield, made plotting our course a business of taking cross bearings every fifteen minutes and straining our eyes through the night glasses for the first loom of the next light. A nerve-wracking process.

The convoy reached Bari one and a half days after leaving Sicily. The town was a shambles of shattered buildings. But the harbour presented the worst scene of destruction. The floor of the main basin was littered with wrecked ships, some on their sides, some sitting upright, only their masts and funnels showing above water. One remarkable sight was a complete Liberty ship, literally plastered against a quay wall, like some grotesque Bas-relief. What tremendous explosion had caused such desolation?

"Bari Harbour 1943"

"Last night there was a heavy enemy air raid on the port of Bari, Southern Italy. There were some Allied losses".

That bare announcement, about the size of a lost and found advert in the press, concealed the worst Allied shipping disaster in the European theatre of war. At the same time it was one of the best kept secrets of the war as the British Government immediately ordered the 30 years rule of censorship to apply to the entire episode. So it only came into the public domain in December 1973.

During the raid 17 ships were sunk, many more damaged, causing 2,000 casualties among servicemen and the civilian population. Two ships collided, exploded and rained shrapnel and, more horrifically, mustard gas, over the whole area. This, mixed with high octane petrol instantly ignited into vast sheets of flame, giving off dense smoke and choking poisonous fumes. During the half-hour that the raid lasted, 100 German bombers coming in at low altitude scored many direct hits in the crowded harbour. It was only the beginning of the holocaust –.

The 9,000 ton SS *John Harvey* (Liberty) was moored next to SS *John Morley* (Liberty) stern first to the mole in a line along with several other ships. *John Harvey* carried mustard gas, *John Morley* ammunition and petrol. *John Morley* broke loose, drifted out of control and began to edge towards *John Harvey*. The crews sensing the danger began to jump overboard but had no time to abandon ship before they collided and the most tremendous explosion occurred. One of the naval ships whose crew did sterling work was a Hunt Class Destroyer HMS *Scotland*. She was lifted out of the water by the explosion and her upper decks scoured by the blast. The funnel was squashed flat, deck fittings ripped off and huge pieces of the disintegrating ships rained down together with a torrent of water. The Captain (Lt-Commander J.V. Wilkinson D.S.C) was badly wounded in the face and the situation was being repeated in the harbour to greater or lesser degree. In addition, a huge tidal wave was created, which drowned men trying to swim to safety. The harbour installations and buildings in the ancient city of Bari were demolished.

The crew of the *Zetland* along with other survivors worked tirelessly for many hours to blast fires out on surviving ships using explosives and re-mooring them. I do not know if any of them ever received awards for bravery, but perhaps they were just some more of war's "forgotten heroes".

My little convoy entered Bari one week later to this scene of devastation. We discharged our 90 Octane petrol, all 12,000 tons thro' a floating pipeline to the mole and along temporary lines to shore. My vivid memory of Bari is of the entire Liberty ship hull "plastered" in Bas-relief against the harbour wall.

Away to the North, we could hear the rumble of the guns, as the German army, under Kesselring, fought its desperate rearguard struggle in the mountainous country. Italy was being won, but at a price.

A British Army Major boarded to supervise the discharge of cargo.

"Dunno if we've got the storage tanks for all of it", he announced cheerfully, "But we'll try".

Much to our relief *British Patience* was Commodore ship on our return trip to Port Augusta. There were only the two of us, as the cargo ships took much longer to unload.

We sailed in a big convoy from Sicily, bound for the States. This time we passed close to the islands of Lampedusa and Pantellaria, which had been bombed so severely by the Allies. No sign of this was visible from five miles off, but it was easy to imagine the destruction, after seeing Bari.

On 5th May, just after passing Oran, the convoy started doing Emergency turns. It was 2.50 am on a dark, windless morning. The TBS began its urgent, fragmentary speech. There came a dull explosion from the far side of the convoy, and the TBS burst into life. An excited voice, hoarse with strain was saying:

"This is Jig One. Jig One calling. I have been torpedoed. Jig Two take over. Jig Two take over – " Silence.

A D.E. getting a whole torpedo to itself, would not have a cat in hell's chance of survival. We waited for the attack to develop. Depth charges boomed at intervals, but the convoy steamed steadily on. Nothing further transpired, and no merchant ships were sunk. Were the Germans beginning to crack at last? I thought of the earlier days in the Med. when whole convoys were wiped out in the effort to reach Malta.

Things were starting to improve.

5

THE LONG VOYAGE

From the Mediterranean, *San Vito* went to New York and loaded for U.K. This time we looked forward to the prospect of leave, for the ship was due her "Guarantee Dry-docking". This is a free overhaul, for a new ship, paid for by the builders. On 27th May, 1944, we left the States for home. Crossing the Grand Banks, we had the usual summer fog, which lasted for several days. Days when the Captain had practically no sleep. This is a problem at sea, which has never been resolved. Tradition and the rules of shipping companies say that the Master shall be on the bridge when navigating in fog. But the academic question is, how long can a man stay on his feet, in charge of a vessel, and retain his judgment and swiftness of reaction? One day, three days? No one looking at a shipmaster's red-rimmed eyes, at his face drawn with fatigue, could but doubt his ability to deal with the sudden emergency, which would loom out of the fog, at any time. Yet the first thing a Marine Court would ask, if there was an accident, would be "Was the Master on the bridge?" No matter how exhausted he might be, he had to be there.

On the morning of 6th June, the ship's radio broadcast the Normandy Landings. As if to celebrate the occasion, the fog lifted. The Captain went below for a well earned sleep. The ship's company were in high spirits. The war was going our way at last. We were homeward bound and who knows, maybe the flinty heart of the Super would melt a little and we would get some leave.

Again we carried planes. They were P.38s – Lockheed Lightnings. Twin engined fighters with extra fuel tanks. They were to be used for the escorting of the massive Flying Fortress daylight raids. Perhaps some of them were destined to fly to Ploesti. Fourteen days after leaving the States *San Vito* tied up at Stanlow, in the

Manchester Ship Canal, after offloading the planes at Ellesmere Port a few miles below Stanlow. The weather was marvellous, high summer in England. With leave in the offing life was sweet.

Soon *San Vito* was on the blocks of Number Six Dry-dock, in Cammell Lairds, Birkenhead. Her tanks were cleaned, her crew paid off and her officers ready to go on leave. Next day I was at home in Scotland with a whole week's leave to come. I returned to the ship engaged, our intention was to be married at the end of the year.

"Only two more trips, darling" I said as I kissed her goodbye.

When I mentioned this happy prospect to Ken Spencer, the rubicund Second Mate, his usually happy face clouded.

"I wouldn't bank on it Steve. The new charts just came aboard. They're for all over the world".

Since our normal charts covered only the Western Hemisphere this was suspicious.

Now one of the surprising things of the war occurred. *San Vito* instead of sailing for the States went back up to Stanlow, and loaded for London, via Loch Ewe. At any time, a ship could be diverted, requisitioned or otherwise mucked about in this way. This was especially true of tankers, whose cargoes were inevitably petroleum products of one kind or another. The Captains themselves knew no more than their crews what their future movements were likely to be. As always the "Galley Wireless" was busy.

The trip round the Coast was similar to that made in *San Amado*. Save that there were no E-boats, no bombers. Only the minefields. And the rumbling of the V.1 Rockets high overhead, as they made their way upriver to London. My only experience of these mon-strous blind engines of destruction came in Tilbury a few days later. I had been to the Shipping Office for Captain Smith, and was standing in the crowded station waiting for my train to Grays. I heard a throaty rumbling roar but paid little heed, as I was reading a newspaper. A voice from along the platform roused me from my perusal of local events. It was a warden, beckoning frantically from the door of a shelter.

"Oi! D'you want to get yourself killed? It's cut out you know!"

I realised two things immediately. The bomb was now silent, on its way to the ground. And the station was deserted, save for my friend of the voice. Everyone had dived into the shelters. As I made to follow a tremendous detonation shook the platform beneath my feet.

"Half a mile away, that one" said the warden. He grinned cheerfully at my white face.

"Does this happen often?" I asked.

"Oh yes" he replied.

He began to regale me with tales of what happened in Croydon last week, in Piccadilly the other day.

"Thanks very much" I said "But I'll stay at sea — its safer"

I wasn't so glad to be at sea a few days later, when I swiped a channel buoy with San Vito. I was on watch on a beautiful summer evening, about ten thirty. The convoy was strung out in two long columns. San Vito was second ship in the port column. On her starboard beam was an old Shell tanker, the Clam. The two leaders were coasters. As we approached Number 21 Buoy, off the Berwickshire coast, the tide was setting down on the buoy. My next ahead, a little ship called the Rother nipped round the buoy with a neat zigzag. I thought I had better follow suit, for the column astern of me would gradually run inside the buoy and I had no idea how far it was safe to go out of the swept channel. In my ignorance I tried to emulate the Rother. But my ship was a twelve thousand ton tanker and you can't throw that around like a coaster. I managed to get the buoy on my port bow, but to my horror it advanced inexorably towards San Vito's hull. I could do nothing but stare at the thing. With a resounding clang it slammed alongside just forward of the bridge, scraped horribly along the hull, before San Vito swept it under her bottom. I rang "Stop" on the Telegraph, with some vague idea of preventing the buoy chain from getting entangled with the propeller.

Captain Smith was on the bridge in seconds. To my relief he wasted no time in telling me his opinion of stupid young mates, but quickly got the situation under control. Once this was achieved he said, mildly,

"Always watch the tide, Mr. Stevenson. Very tricky it can be".

I had received a salutary lesson, a blow to my ego.

The Pentland Firth was a channel of exquisite beauty and awful loneliness. It seemed that no human being could live on the bleak moorland which swept away from the forbidding cliffs. At 11.30p.m. in July it was still daylight up there. The sky a beautiful pale blue, shading to a pearly green towards the northern horizon. The sea was like glass, broken only by the prows of the ships forging their way through.

Round Cape Wrath and Duncansby Head we sailed, through the Minches and came to anchor in the late evening in Loch Long. Over towards the Greenock shore lay two of the largest ships in the world. The *Queen Elizabeth* and the *Aquitania* just in from America with more troops.

It had been an interesting trip to London. The Thames had been full of invasion ships. From ungainly L.S.Ts. and the little "Jeep" cargo ships built specially for the landings because of their shallow draft, to the inevitable *Liberties* and C.2s, on whose sides were painted black code numbers to assist in the efficient discharge of cargo. It had been possible to gauge the vastness of the operation from the numbers of ships setting out for the Continent.

By 18th July we were at sea again, bound for America. Another routine convoy, boring in its monotony and safety. I almost wished that something would attack us just for a change. The U-boats were having a lean time. Though we had heard of the Schnorkel Tube, which meant a U-boat need not surface to charge batteries, the Hunter/killer groups of allied warships ensured the safe passage of convoy after convoy.

Six days from New York we were detached from the convoy and ordered to Guantanamo Bay, Cuba. For the first few days our escort was a Martin Mariner flying boat, which visited us daily to see if we were OK. As we neared Cuba we got a blimp escort. I had not seen one since early '42, on the Eastern Seaboard. It was like meeting an old friend. The situation at sea must have been well under control if so much attention could be lavished on one ship.

Late on 4th August *San Vito* sailed between Crooked Island and Long Island in the Eastern Bahamas. The next day, Saturday, she slid through the entrance to Guantanamo Bay, the United States naval base in southern Cuba. To the surprise and delight of everyone mail was waiting. After taking some fresh vegetable stores, *San Vito* sailed that evening in a tiny convoy for Curacao. By 8th August she was loading petrol in Bullen Bay, at the Western end of the Island. It was good to be back in the Caribbean again. The weather is as pleasant as can be found anywhere in the world. There is always the refreshing wind of the South East Trades, to keep it from being unbearably hot. And Curacao, with its smell compounded of petroleum and dusty vegetation, was exciting.

From Curacao we went to Trinidad, some three days away. The galley wireless was at work again. The petrol we had loaded was low grade.

"This lot won't be for home lads. What's the bet it'll be South America or Africa?" There were no takers.

It appeared we would be in Trinidad for a few days. Captain Smith granted shore leave. Trinidad is a lovely island and Port of Spain a fine city, nestling as it does at the foot of blue mountains, whose peaks almost touch the creamy cotton wool clouds. A curious feature of the Caribbean is this formation of clouds over each island or group of islands. This is caused by warm air currents from the land rising and condensing the moisture in the atmosphere. The resulting clouds are usually Alto-Cumulus, the fleecy cotton-wool clouds of fine weather.

From Monday to Friday SanVito lay in the beautiful roadstead off Port of Spain, and at 2.30p.m. her anchor came home to its hawse pipe and was secured by its steel claw on the chain. As she steamed through the Boca Del Dragone her destination was anybody's guess. Later it leaked out. It was Durban, Natal. Three days later off Pernambuco, we struck out across the desolate wastes of the South Atlantic.

The sea, when one is out of sight of land, looks very much the same anywhere in the world. But the South Atlantic I felt, was more vast, more pitiless. Perhaps because as a navigating officer I knew the tremendous distances between us and any land. Perhaps it was because, in the North Atlantic the "Ship population" was so much greater, that the chances of being picked up, if torpedoed, were good.

But now we were really on our own. The deep swells rolled up incessantly out of the South East, as the ship rolled on day after day. There was not even a bird to be seen. The endless days were relieved by the exciting news broadcast on the radio.

23rd August – Paris liberated. Rumania accepts Russian Peace Terms.

31st August – Allies reach Somme. Russians reach Ploesti.

1st September – Americans reach Verdun. Russians reach Bucharest.

Somewhere between 1st September and 11th September we crossed the Equator.

As we neared "The Line" preparations were put in hand for meeting King Neptune and his court. The canvas swimming bath was rigged on the main deck, and Chippie fixed up a devilish contraption over one edge. It was a chair in the style of the old-fashioned ducking stool. It looked very sinister. We novitiates had a few qualms as "The Day" dawned.

At nine o'clock, Neptune and his court arrived from under the Focsle Head. Splendidly arrayed, with a lifeboat grapnel for a trident, a cardboard crown bearing the legend Corn Flakes, and a beard and wig of oakum, he was a most imposing figure. No less impressive was his retinue, with the two most brawny A.B.s as "policemen". Once a novice got into the grasp of those two, he went quietly.

The royal herald stepped forward.

"Know ye, by these presents, that all manner of mariners, when crossing the line for the first time, shall do homage to His Marine Majesty, Neptunus Rex. After the fashion decreed from time immemorial; the said mariner then to be admitted to the Honourable Company of Shellbacks".

Then in an aside to the Captain.

"Permission to carry on sir?" The Captain nodded gravely.

"Very good. My compliments to His Marine Majesty. May I ask Him to call on me for refreshments, after the Ceremonies?"

"Cor, Ta very – I mean, thank you very much, sir!"

Now came the period of pursuit and capture as hapless novices were tracked down. There was no escape. After a token struggle, I went quietly. I had already seen what happened to those who didn't. Secured between two burly "Policemen" they were beaten into submission with long cardboard truncheons.

Finally there were eight of us, waiting with mounting

apprehension for what was to come. Since I was the only officer I was taken first. My name was called. I stepped forward.

"Kneel before the King!" A large galley "Kid" full of porridge laced with rum and sugar, was placed in front of me. A huge ladle was dipped into it, and offered to me. As I opened my mouth to taste it, an expert flick of the wrist spread the gooey sticky mess right over my head. Gasping and spluttering I was hauled to the "Chair". A mixture of soft soap, flour and water was liberally brushed on my face by the "Barber" using a ten inch paint brush. In spite of the struggles I was pinioned hand and foot by the "Policemen".

With a three foot wooden Razor this was scraped off my face, none too delicately. Then,

"Whoosh!" The barber released the chair, and I toppled backwards into the pool where I was grabbed by two more attendants and ducked three times. I came up half drowned, to find the second victim thrashing beside me.

The Ship's Bell rang suddenly. At that very moment she was crossing the Line. It was my first time in the Southern Hemisphere.

When the last novice had been ducked, we were lined up before Neptune, and solemnly presented with a scroll, liberally embellished with dolphins and bosomy mermaids, entwined in seaweed. The legend thereon went something like this.

COURT OF NEPTUNUS REX "SAN VITO" EQUATOR

Know ye, all Creatures of the Deep, All Fishes, Dolphins, Mermaidens, Octupuses and Sea Serpents: That D Stevenson having successfully passed the examination by ordeal on board the above vessel on the Line. 10th September 1944, is now admitted to the Honourable Company of Shellbacks.

Signed
Neptunus Rex.

Then came the turn of Neptune and his minions. With wild yells they disappeared into the swimming bath, after a pell mell chase round the decks. A hilarious and successful end to an enjoyable morning. True to his word, the Captain invited Neptune and his Court (otherwise the Chief Steward and some of the Crew) up to his day cabin for a well earned peg.

Twenty one days after leaving Trinidad an armed trawler came out to meet us from Simonstown. She escorted us round the Cape of Good Hope, dashing in the process our hopes of going into Cape Town for bunkers. We steamed down past Simonstown, into the Agulhas Current. This mighty rush of water is caused by the flow of one ocean into the other, round Cape Agulhas, "Needle Point" so named by the Portuguese. The waters off the Cape had been mined by the captured British merchantman *Speybank*. We, of course did not know of this. All we did know was that our sailing instructions were very explicit as to the course we should follow when rounding the Cape.

Now we had the mainland of South Africa on our port side, as we headed into the Indian Ocean, past Port Elizabeth and East London, heading for Durban. It had been a long, weary trip, one of the longest sea passages I had ever made. On 16th September, thirty one days from Trinidad, *San Vito* attempted the entrance to Durban, but it was too rough and windy. She steamed at slow speed up and down off shore all night. At dawn it was hardly better, though the wind had moderated a little. At 7.15 the Pilot boarded and we ran the breakwaters with the Bluff on our port hand in pouring rain. By nine o'clock the ship was tied up at the oil berth. Across the bay we could make out through the rain, the silhouettes of Durban's many fine buildings. On the quayside beautifully muscled Zulus manhandled the pipeline flexibles, chanting all the time. Soon the hoses were bucking and swaying rhythmically as our cargo flowed ashore to the distant tank farm. Once in Manchester I asked the Cargo Supervisor: – "which tank?"

"That one" he said, indicating what to me was a ridiculously small tank.

"All of it in there?" I asked incredulously.

"Sure" he answered, "It holds 15,000 tons"

During our stay in Durban it rained all the time and we were unable to have a ride in one of the famous rickshaws. We merely strolled up the main streets, all of which had canopies over the shop fronts, an idea which could be copied with advantage over here.

One thing which disturbed me was the evidence of colour bar. There were separate drinking fountains, separate toilets, separate seats on public transport. Being a bi-lingual country every thing was written in Afrikaans and English.

In the evening "Sparks", who had visited Durban before on a Clan boat, took us to "The Playhouse" a blend of pub, restaurant and cinema. It was designed on the lines of an old English Coaching inn, with a courtyard surrounded by a gallery, off which were rooms. In the square of the yard and on the galleries one could have a meal or a drink. Opposite the entrance to the yard was the cinema. It was a popular place with "Durbanites" at that time. Overhead clouds moved slowly across a starlit sky.

"Look, Sparks, it's stopped raining" I said.

He laughed "How d'you make that out?"

"Look – the stars are out"

"That's the ceiling, man"

And so it was. A beautifully engineered idea, which gave one the impression of sitting out under the open sky.

We sailed two days later. As we left the docks a lady dressed all in white, singing most sweetly in a contralto voice:

> "Now is the hour when we must say Goodbye
> Now we are sailing, far across the sea"

We gave her a good cheer and were rewarded by her waving and blowing kisses.

Back aboard ship, rumours as to our next port flew thick and fast. Return to Curacao was a pious hope, soon to be dashed. Once we got to sea we knew the worst. Our destination was Abadan, in the Persian Gulf. To a sailor "Abadan" spells "Hell". Forty five miles up the Shatt-al-Arab River at the head of the Gulf, it is in summer one of the hottest places in the world. Temperatures of 107 degrees are usual, and up to 120 in the shade is fairly common. Couple this with tremendously high humidity, and the ship becomes a steel inferno. In the Merchant Navy anyone slightly dotty is said to have a "touch of the Abadans".

Since we could make no better of it, we resigned ourselves to re-crossing the Equator and listening to the gruesome accounts of those of the crew who had already been to Abadan. So terrible was this place that I felt I must see it, if only to die of heat stroke in the attempt.

One sand-hazed day we passed Cape Guardafui, the Eastern tip of Socotra, a British possession. It was remarkable how the key points of land in the world belonged to Great Britain. I went over them in my mind. Leaving England to go to the Far East, one passed Gibraltar, Malta, Cyprus, Alexandria (Once British), the Suez Canal, acquired by Mr. Disraeli in a brilliant business deal. The Red Sea had its share of things British. The Straits of Bab-el-Mandeb, at the southern end were guarded by Perim Island, while the opposite shore was British Somaliland. The Gulf of Aden was dominated by the "Barren Rocks", with Socotra on the African shore. All the way to the Far East it was the same. Ceylon, at the Southern tip of India, the Maldive and Laccadive Islands in the Indian Ocean, followed by the Nicobars. Then Penang at the top of the Malacca Straits with Singapore at the bottom. Our Empire building forefathers, though ridiculed today, were men of vision.

San Vito crawled up the Hadramaut Coast of southern Arabia. The land on the chart was overprinted with the legend "Hostile Tribesman". Pity any vessel which ever ran aground on such an inhospitable coast. Dry barren cliffs, perpetually bathed in sand haze. Then we were in the Gulf of Oman, steering for the Quoins, the entrance proper of the Gulf. The sea was an intense blue and flat calm, relieved by the white triangles of distant dhows. How these craft sailed in such calm seas was a marvel. But the huge lateen sail was made to catch every ghost of a breeze, and use it to propel the exquisitely shaped hull through the water.

These dhows, mainly Arabian, traded from the Gulf ports of Muscat, Bahrain, Kuwait and Bushire, to Dar-es-Salaam and Zanzibar, East Africa, and as far afield as India and Ceylon. They would carry dates, salt, dried fish, kerosene, guns and slaves. For slavery still flourished in this part of the world.

When the *San Ernesto* was torpedoed in the Indian Ocean by a Japanese submarine, the survivors sailed in open lifeboats for 28 days before they reached the Maldive Islands. It was a voyage of pure unadulterated hell. Thirst and heat were the main ingredients of their torture. At home, they were given up as "Missing". They made it, and after some days in the kindly care of the islanders of a tiny atoll, they were taken in a dhow to Mali Atoll, the Capital of the Maldives. There was a radio station here and their families were overjoyed to learn of their safety. From Mali Atoll they sailed for Colombo. The voyage took ten to eleven days, and the Second Officer said afterwards he did not know how the navigation was done. The Knockador, or Master of the dhow, had an ancient sextant and book of tables, but did not use them. All alterations of course were made at night. The Master would sit cross-legged by the helmsman, gazing intently at the stars. After about an hour he would give a call. All hands woke up from where they lay around the decks and to an Arab chant laid the big lateen sail over on the other tack, before going back to sleep. It was uncanny, unrealistic navigation, but it fetched Adam's Peak and Colombo Harbour out of the sea, right ahead, one damp morning.

That night I was on watch. The night was like black silk, and so dark that sea and sky merged into one, without any horizon. The translucent, emerald fire of the bow wave glimmered on the hull and deck houses. Overhead the stars were giant sequins on a velvet gown. On such a night, the faintest gleam of light on the shore would be seen.

I walked up and down humming to myself and thinking of girl friend and home. Occasionally I paused to stare right round the horizon. Soon it would be Midnight and I would be relieved by the Second Mate. It would be a pity to turn in on such a fine night. My eye was caught by the flash of a light. I stared, unblinking, waiting for it to show again. Yes. There it was. ONE, TWO, THREE. It was only the "Loom", which is the beam of the light as it shows above the curvature of the Earth. But we were fifty odd miles from the Quoins on which stood the only lighthouse for hundreds of miles. I went into the chartroom to verify our dead reckoning. Was it possible that three skilled navigators should be so far out? Going back to the bridge wing I counted the "Characteristic" of the flashes. Sure enough it was the Quoins I was seeing. But on the charts its visibility was 18 miles. I called the Captain, and he checked the light, before looking up the Sailing Directions for the Persian Gulf.

"Due to greatly increased refraction, lights and land will often be seen at much greater distances than can normally be expected". There was our answer. When we did get a good check on our position it was found that the distance I had first seen the light was 47 miles − 29 miles further than normal.

By daylight *San Vito* had rounded the Quoins and was at last in the Persian Gulf. She closed the land toward Khor Kuwai, the Naval Signal Station, to identify herself. I felt sorry for the men stationed in such a barren place. Surrounded by blistering cliffs whose rocks gave out, in the night, the heat which they had stored during the day, their lives must have been miserable.

The instructions we got were to proceed, not to Abadan, but to Bahrain Island.

"Good Luck" Our Aldis lamp stuttered as we turned away on course. At least we had a reprieve from Abadan this time. I studied the chart of the Persian Gulf. Bounded on its Eastern side by the arid cruel peaks of Baluchistan, rising to nearly 4,000 feet its Eastern waters are deep, its shores steep too and with few anchorages. Several islands, the tops of mountains, lie scattered here and there. They are named "Jezirat" or "Jebel", which means "Island" and "Mountain" respectively in Arabic.

The Western shores of the Gulf are quite different. A maze of coral reefs separates the deep water from the flat Saudi Arabian desert. These coral banks are famed for their pearling. The Arabs who do the fishing eke out a precarious living, for though a pearl of great price is occasionally found, hundreds of oysters must be opened before that one prize is gained.

The Island of Bahrein, some 250 miles up the Gulf, is a coral island. Its capital is Manama, which has as its centre the Sheik's palace. Today there is an airstrip and deepwater loading berths for tankers and cargo vessels, but in 1944 there was only one berth and that was off shore.

With every mile the ship moved up the Gulf the temperature rose. Yet this was October. What on earth was it like in summer?

As darkness fell on October 7th we anchored off the lights of Bahrein to wait for daylight. At dawn, the berthing master came out and we moved slowly down a narrow channel in the coral. Our berth was a four square structure of wooden piles, connected to the shore by a submarine pipeline. The berthing master, Captain Shotton, who also doubled as cargo supervisor, did a fine job, without the help of tugs. There are several deep water berths and tugs to help the giant ships of modern times.

Our interest was centred on our next port. When it was learned that it was Suez we were overjoyed. When we got that far, they were bound to send us through the Canal to load in Haifa for home. It was in a cheerful frame of mind that the ship sailed down past the Quoins, three wedge shaped islands whose barrenness is only relieved by a red and white striped lighthouse. Down the Gulf of Oman, past Ras-al-Hadd, the most Easterly point of Arabia and into the Gulf of Aden. Thank goodness we had seen the last of that lot. How narrowly we had escaped from Abadan.

Through Hell's Gates, the Straits of Bab-el-Mandeb and up the Red Sea. Surely all shipping which has passed this way must have worn a hole in the sea. But no, it was still the same, intensely blue and sparkling in the sunshine. The crew were as brown as berries, after many weeks in the sun. It seems wonderful to people in this country to live under perpetual sunshine. But it had its snags. In the tremendous heat we sweated profusely. This led to prickly heat, a pink rash, which soon breaks into tiny septic spots. It is very itchy and painful and usually appears on the chest and back as well as the crotch and armpits. We waddled around like so many ducks, our legs and bodies smothered in calamine lotion, our only remedy.

On Monday 23rd October 1944 the ship docked at Suez Oil Terminal at 5.15 p.m. As usual it was miles from the town. It had one advantage. We were not plagued by the "Bumboat men" who swarmed in the port itself, selling silks, Turkish delight, and postcards so filthy they were ludicrous. I found out where the flies go in Winter − Egypt − with Suez as the main transit camp. They came in their millions. Black, sticky, filthy. Insect sprays killed some, but not nearly enough. How the Eighth Army coped with the Afrika Korps and flies was a wonder.

I visited an Egyptian dentist while the ship was in Suez. A front tooth needed filling. 1 went in the Agency car, down innumerable back streets full of noisy children, to a house on the first floor of a block of flats. As soon as I was out of the car I was surrounded by the children, ragged and dirty, crying,

"Backsheesh Effendi − Backsheesh!"

The dentist, a lithe and swarthy Egyptian said after he had examined me,

"You must come for treatment – six appointments!"

"I can't " I said "I'm a ship's officer. Can't you take it out?"

So he did, most painfully. I lost a large part of my upper gum. I've had teeth pulled in many places, but that extraction really hurt.

"Did you have to be so cruel?" I asked. He sneered.

"You British – so soft".

I felt like hanging one on his supercilious jaw.

San Vito's cargo was kerosene. She discharged part cargo in Suez, and at 11.20a.m. on Thursday, 26th October she left for Aden. Five days later she called briefly at Steamer Point, for routine instructions and by dark on Tuesday, 31st October she was creeping up the Arabian Coast bound for Bahrein, once more. By 7th November she had reached Bahrein where she loaded a special "kero" cargo, for of all places, Abadan. So she finally got right up the Gulf, almost by the back door.

Twenty six hours after leaving Bahrein the Pilot boarded from the gleaming white cutter of the Basrah Port Authority off the entrance to the Shatt-el-Arab River. As the ship entered Rooka Channel, a dredged passage between sandbanks, a strange smell assailed our nostrils. Compounded of sand, petroleum and burning camel dung, it stamped "Abadan" on my senses as vividly as fish and chips does England.

At 4.15 p.m. on Wednesday 15th November 1944, the ship lay at anchor in Bawarda Reach, the Quarantine and waiting Anchorage for ships using Abadan. It is some two miles below Abadan.

Abadan is the perfect example of what man can make out of nothing in his efforts to extract riches from the earth. Before 1908 it was a semi-tidal swamp, lying between the Shatt-el-Arab and Bahar Rivers, infested with mosquitoes. The Anglo Persian oil Company decided it would be a good spot to build what was to become the largest oil refinery in the world. A bund was constructed to keep the rivers back, jetties were built out and the refinery rose, a complex silver structure of cracking towers, distillation units and miles of piping. A power house was built, tank farms and houses for employees constructed. By clever landscaping and constant irrigation a garden city gradually grew round the refinery. During the second world war Abadan supplied the needs of our armies in India, Burma and the Eastern Hemisphere.

All over tea-time we fought off the bumboats which swarmed alongside from the Iraqi shore. The river from Basrah to the sea, was the boundary between Iraq and Iran. The time in Iraq was one hour behind that in Iran; so that when the ship lay in the river she was on Iraq time and when alongside a jetty she was on Iran time.

At five thirty, in sweltering heat the Assistant Harbour Master boarded to pilot *San Vito* to her berth. We went on stations. A wind blew out of the north, the oven blast of some great furnace.

"Is it always like this, Pilot?" asked Captain Smith.

"This is nothing Captain. At least its dry just now. You should be up here during the Monsoon, when the humidity gets up to Ninety per cent. Oh, yes. It's fine right now!"

Whew! If this is fine, heaven help us if we ever did come up in the hot season.

The ship berthed at Number 22 Jetty. There were twenty six jetties on the river bank, including a dry cargo wharf. Number 19 to 26 were white oil or "Spirit" jetties, where the fire hazard was greatest. The remaining jetties were for "black" oils and miscellaneous purposes.

The river was a grey brown flood running at a good three knots. There was little tidal effect. Only at Springs did the tide change to "Flood" and then only for an hour or so. Across the river the sun set quickly, dipping behind the lines of bluish green date palms silhouetting the Iraqi shore. Darkness fell fairly rapidly and the lights began to shine in the brief dusk. Like some huge science fiction fantasy, columns of lights towered to the sky. The flames from the waste gas towers glared redly. Surrounded on all sides by the limitless desert, it was the anachronism, the impossibility, the modern miracle that was Abadan.

I went on deck to supervise the start of the loading.

By next afternoon *San Vito* had finished loading and was heading downriver bound for Aden. Now most of us knew, or if we did not know, we suspected that the ship was "Out East" indefinitely. This knowledge depressed us for some days, but the natural optimism of the sailor soon began to rise. At least we had never been to Aden. Maybe it would be not so bad after all.

The trip down the Shatt-el-Arab was full of interest. Navigation of narrow waters has always held a fascination for me. The "Shatt" is the outflow of the two great Biblical rivers, Euphrates and Tigris, after their confluence at Basrah. From Basrah to the sea is approximately ninety miles and from Abadan forty five. This first stretch from Abadan to the bend at Kabda was eleven miles. It was dead straight, reminding me of the Suez Canal, whose entrance I had seen on the previous trip. Then came the S bends of Kabda and Kasba, leading into Kasba Reach, another straight of six miles. A further bend brought the ship into Fao Reach, named after the Dredging Station at Fao.

In the days before the cutting of the Suez Canal there had been a great dream of running a railway from Port Said, across the desert to a port on the Persian Gulf at Fao. Steamers would run a service from Europe to Port Said and from Fao to India. Passengers would travel in comfort across the desert by rail. But De Lesseps cut his canal, and Fao remained what it always would be. A tiny nucleus of civilisation, perched between the desert and the sea, the dredging station and home of the Basrah Port Authority's Dredging Service. It was connected to Basrah a hundred miles away by a good straight road.

Eleven miles below Fao we signalled our name to the Traffic Control, an ancient steamer, manned by a British Officer and Iraqi crew. It was moored close to a tide gauge and its function was to give tidal information to the ships about to use Rooka Channel. This was necessary as Rooka was barely navigable by deep laden tankers, owing to silting. It was kept open by the efforts of the dredgers operating from Fao.

That November morning there was plenty of water for *San Vito* and by lunch on 20th November she was well on her way down the Gulf, heading South East for the Quoins and the Indian Ocean. Life on board settled down to routine. Boring, frustrating in its monotony of eternal sun and sparkling blue sea.

Seven days later around noon on Monday, 27th November the jagged peaks of Aden reared out of the sea, fine on our starboard bow. By evening we had anchored in the roads, awaiting a berth. At ten next day our cargo was pulsing through a floating pipeline to the tanks at Steamer Point. There was no shore leave for me. I was kept busy with cargo and the thought of going ashore by boat in the heat of the afternoon was not inviting.

The following afternoon we sailed from Aden. Our destination, Djibouti, British Somaliland. Here was a real outpost of Empire. A small colony on the edge of the desert. San Vito tied up at the oil wharf, which had been made out of the overturned hull of an old merchant ship. An extraordinary sight.

We left Aden on 30th November and arrived in Djibouti at dawn next day. It took us all that day and part of the night to discharge our allotted cargo. Djibouti was a big dhow port. Away up the harbour lay scores of those graceful craft. Some were real beauties, particularly those of the Red Sea. In contrast with the Dhows of the Indian Ocean and Persian Gulf, they are smaller, with longer, more rakish lines. Very sleek and fast, for they run guns and slaves across the Red Sea, from Yemen, Sudan and other parts of the African and Arabian Coasts. To see one gliding out of the harbour, white hull flamingo pink in the sunset, her full lateen sail curving to the invisible, scarce perceptible breeze, was to see something out of the past.

On Saturday, 2nd December San Vito sailed for Port Sudan, to get rid of the last of her cargo. On the way the crew gas freed tanks numbers four to seven. Several days later, on 5th December the ship tied up at the oil berth of Port Sudan. It was 6.45a.m. a beautiful dawn. Nothing happened for about an hour. This was unusual, for the normal practice of oil companies is to get the cargo started before the ship is tied up properly. But here there was no one, no one that is unless you counted three Arabs fast asleep in the shade of a pipeline. The ship's officers stared anxiously across a shimmering dusty plain to the distant township. All that connected the jetty with this civilisation was a light, narrow gauge railway running into the blue.

Presently a speck appeared on the track in the far distance. Was it a train? There was no smoke. Was it electric? Not fast enough. Was it motor-driven? No noise. Before our astonished eyes it resolved itself into a small four wheeled trolley surmounted by a snow white awning, richly baubled and fringed. It was pushed by four gleaming back Nubians. Beneath the awning sat two white men. As the trolley rolled to a stop at the ship's side, the two men descended with immense dignity. Tall, sunburned, and – one sported a monocle.

"My sainted Aunt Fanny!" gasped the Second Mate. "Now I've seen everything". The men turned out to be the cargo supervisor and the Installation manager.

Actually, in spite of our initial revulsion at their use of human "horses" they were decent chaps. When I asked about the trolley they replied

"You know old boy, these boys rather enjoy it. We never have any lack of volunteers for the job. Its easier than working all day".

That afternoon I went ashore for a few hours. Port Sudan is on the West side of the Red Sea, about halfway down. It is one of the hottest places in the world, being on a par with Abadan, though the heat was dry when we visited it. It was a small clean town of white washed buildings whose walls reflected the glare of the sun till my eyes ached. A tiny business centre, and rows of Arab shops and stores. These latter were literally "holes in the wall" yet they sold an amazing variety of goods. My eye was attracted to one shop, full of exquisitely carved ivory. There was a chess set of ivory and ebony, and a pair of beautiful ivory elephants, carved on the curve of the tusk. If I had the time to haggle I expect I could have obtained one or the other. But time was short, and I had to leave them.

At 7.20 a.m. next morning the ship sailed through the reefs guarding Port Sudan and set her course for Aden, where she would get her routing instructions. We did not need them. For we knew in our hearts that it would be the Gulf once more.

On 18th December *San Vito's* anchor plunged to the muddy bottom of Bawarda Reach in a heavy rain storm. This was an historical event in Abadan where the rainfall is practically Nil. It was unreal to see Abadan, the hottest place in the world, looking like Manchester on a wet Sunday. It was chilly too.

Captain Smith, by some means, was able to get some Christmas fare while we were in port. Christmas was going to be a right cheerful "do".

We loaded at Number 26 jetty. The cargo supervisor was able to tell us our port of discharge was Colombo, Ceylon. The morale of the ship sank to zero. But oil companies have no conscience. We had signed on for the trip so we had to do it.

At 5 a.m. on Saturday, 23rd December, the engine room telegraph rang "Full Away on Passage" after we had dropped the pilot off Rooka. It was raining heavily and blowing up a moderate gale from the North West. We might as well have been in the North Sea, so cold was it. At tea time on Christmas Eve Jezirat Tunb was sighted through the rain. At least we were on the right road out of the Gulf. But after tea, someone got out a guitar, and the mouth organ, and soon a merry band was "visiting", singing Christmas carols. I say merry. What each man thought he kept to himself. Everyone was bluffing, but in the act of bluff, he forgot now depressed he was. For the time being.

On Christmas morning 1944 it was still raining heavily. The Quoins were rounded at 7.30 a.m. and the ship put on course down the Gulf of Oman. Now the wind, which had been rising steadily for two days, backed from North East right round to South and blew a regular gale. So rough was it that the engines were eased a few revolutions. We could have been in the North Atlantic. This was very rough weather for the Persian Gulf. It did not affect the appetites for the Christmas dinner, we all had a good feed.

By 27th December we were in the fine weather of the Indian Ocean as the ship steamed on for the coast of India. Two days later we picked up the Burlings, a group of islands just South of Bombay. Soon we were in the traffic route of the Indian coast ten to fifteen miles off shore. New Year's Eve was a day like any other as we steamed southwards past Goa and the red ochre cliffs of Cochin, across the Palk Straits to the Isle of Spices – Ceylon. Aboard, all hands were cheerfully looking forward to a celebration on New Years Day in Colombo. Spirits were high. The ship was off Colombo Harbour at 4.15 p.m. on Monday, 1st January 1945. She anchored in the Roadstead at 6.30 p.m. and lay swinging round her pick till the 4th January. So much for our celebration. At breakfast time the ship was fast at the Oil dock.

Colombo was the real port of romantic oriental fancy. Its wharves and quays filled with tall funnelled Brocklebank ships, with neat little British India coastwise vessel, and as always, the dhows, lying in clusters, like so many brown hens. The waterfront was a pile of handsome Victorian buildings of which the Galle Face Hotel was the finest example. The streets were wide and clean, with many fine shops.

That evening the Mate and I were invited to dinner by the Shell Installation Manager. His house was a large cool bungalow set in a lovely tropic garden. Afterwards we went to a film. The mere fact of doing something so civilised, yet so simple, made the reality of the ship the next day, all the more frustrating.

By Saturday morning Colombo was a blur astern. *SanVito* was en route for Trincomalee, the British Naval Base on the East Coast of Ceylon. It took her two days, round Dondra Head and Point de Galle, till she berthed at Admiralty Pier, Trincomalee.

From Trincomalee, we returned to Number 26 Jetty, Abadan. They must have reserved it for us. A buzz roused the crew from their lethargic acceptance of our boring and miserable lot. Dry-dock! A magic word. But it quickly died and this time we went to Karachi, where we arrived on 31st January. Karachi is now in Pakistan, a fine modern city, with a good harbour.

Like all good officers, the Mate thought it would cut the cost of dry-docking, if he could get the ship painted overside. After running from the previous June, the old lady was a shocking sight. Her sides were a mass of rust, and her bows had great patches and water streaks of discolouration all over them. An Indian contractor offered to do the job in a day, if the ship supplied the paint and stage.

"How much?" asked the Mate.

"Now then, sir. All grey topsides. No boot topping? For you – I make it two hundred rupees"

The Mate did a quick calculation in his head.

"Done" he said.

For the sum of £15.10.0 he got the ship painted round.

The result was ghastly. Great curtains of paint ran and fused with each other, as fifty coolies painted their way round the hull. As much paint went in the water as went on the ship's side. It was a bosun's nightmare. But it covered up the rust. The coolies got one rupee a day. Sweated labour?

On 3rd February we sailed for Bahrein, where we loaded a cargo for Calcutta. It was a very depressed ship's company that rounded the Quoins that trip. Life was becoming deadly monotonous. The food was rapidly deteriorating, due to the ineptitude of the Steward, and the fact that ship's stores were hard to come by, both in Indian ports and in Abadan. We had long since finished the potatoes and were eating "Dehydrated " spuds. These bore no resemblance to potatoes as I knew them, being an unusual shade of green, with flavour to match. We even tried yams, which were all right for a change, but too starchy to last for any period. Prickly heat was rife. So was bad temper. Foot rot had become prevalent among the Engine Room staff, due to walking so much on hot steel plates. If only we could get a break in port for a few weeks, it would make all the difference. Maybe it would come after this trip.

Since our draft of 28'6" was too deep for the Hooghly River, we called at Madras, South East India, to lighten to 24'6", the safe draft for Calcutta.

Once again it was round the tip of Ceylon and up the East Coast into the Bay of Bengal. We left Bahrein on 12th February.. We arrived in Madras on the 25th, to discharge through a floating "Crocodile" pipeline to the shore.

Fifteen days out from Abadan we came up to the Sandheads. This is the pilot station for one of the largest rivers in the world, the mighty Hooghly. At Benares, far to the north, it is called the Ganges and is a holy river. At its confluence with the Bramaputra, it becomes the Hooghly.

It was a glorious morning on Thursday 1st March 1945 when *SanVito* approached the elderly steam vessel which did duty as Pilot Cutter. The big Monsoon swells lifted and dropped her like some graceful seabird, as she made a neat turn round the stern of the tanker and hove to, some distance off. A blue painted whaler smacked into the water. As it became waterborne on the top of a swell, the falls were expertly slipped. Her crew, blue uniformed, red tarbooshed, tossed oars, fended off, and in the twinkling of an eye were pulling strongly towards our pilot ladder.

This was the Bengal Pilot Service, one of the crack Pilotages of the world. One had to be very "pukka" to become apprenticed to this illustrious service.

The Pilot, who had coxed the boat, mounted our ladder in a dignified manner. I saluted smartly as he came over the rail. Behind him came a little fat Indian, carrying a big gladstone bag and on his back, an outsize laundry bag. Our grinning seamen helped him aboard, but he brushed aside their offers to carry his gear and followed the pilot and I round corners and up ladders with an agility which his appearance belied. This was the Pilot's "Tiger" – his personal servant.

With some amusement we watched him at work in the chartroom, which he seemed to have taken over as the Pilot's room. He found his way round a strange ship with no trouble at all, procuring hot water so his master could shave. He stood by with brush and razor, handing each article solemnly to his master as required. The latter, his brick red countenance pinker than ever from his shave, talked incessantly in the loud cultured accents of the old British Raj. Telling Captain Smith about the current at Diamond Harbour, or the siltage in Eden Channel I got the impression that the Hooghly was kept navigable only by the skill and knowledge of its pilots, who, British to the core, loudly proclaimed their abilities and scoffed at any suggestion that Indians could ever learn the river. To give the Bengal Pilots their due, they were skilful pilots in a most treacherous river whose shifting sands and banks could, and often did, change from week to week. But in spite of the fulminations of the British pilots, the job is done today just as efficiently and with far less showmanship by Indian and Pakistani Pilots.

At 7 a.m. *San Vito* bumped her way gently over Eden Bar and proceeded up the muddy estuary of the Hooghly. She had 80 miles to go to reach Buj-Buj one hour before sunset. This would give her time to go alongside before dark. Her crew then had from about six p.m. till midnight to moor the ship. If this seems a long time to tie up a ship let me explain.

The Hooghly River has a "Bore". This is a natural phenomenon where a river has a swift current, many sand banks and its outflow pours into a wide land locked bay or channel. A good example in this country is the Severn Bore, caused by the pressure of the tide flowing up the Bristol Channel to meet and over-ride the swift current of the river itself. Further restrictions and constrictions of the water, by sand banks and bends in the river result in a wall of water, anything from two to ten feet high rushing up the river channel at five to six knots.

So it was with the Hooghly. The distance to Calcutta was 120 miles which gave the Bore a chance to build up into a fearful, devastating wall some fourteen feet high at Howrah Bridge. Buj-Buj was twenty four miles below Calcutta and the Bore was correspondingly reduced. Nevertheless its height on the left bank on which Buj-Buj was situated was two to three feet. On the right bank, where stood nothing of much consequence, it rose to a height of ten to twelve feet.

All ships therefore had to be well moored. Ordinary manila ropes and steel wires would snap like cotton when the Bore passed, and it was before the days of nylon ropes. So we used our anchor chains. The ship was made fast to two buoys at each end in the normal way. Both anchors were then "hung off" and two fifteen fathom "Shackles" of cable lowered into a mooring boat which had a specially adapted bow for handling cable and buoys. These were taken aft for the stern moorings. The ends of the cables were secured to the buoys fore and aft, and, in the case of the bows, the windlass took up the slack and that was that. At the stern the boat secured the ends of the cables to the buoys before passing the remaining ends on board the ship. These were turned up on the mooring bollards by the crew, a task easier to describe than do. The anchor cable was $2^{1}/_{2}$" chain, rusty and intractable. It was also very heavy. To augment the cables on the poop, two six-fold purchases were rigged from the buoys with 24 inch coir springs, and the whole lot hove taut. The blocks of the purchases stood two feet high. It was back-breaking, killing work in the steamy jungle heat. While the crew struggled on, the berthing master was urging them on with horrible tales of mooring bollards being torn completely out of a ship's deck by the strength of the Bore. It was well past midnight when the crew secured the last tackle and collapsed on the deck, sweating like pigs. All but the Berthing Master, who stood in an attitude of tense listening before turning to me.

"The Bore will be here in twenty minutes" he said "Just time for a smoke".

I offered him one. It was permissible to smoke aft of the funnel.

"How can you be so sure of that?" I asked.

For answer he indicated the river, gleaming in the starlight.

"Look at the small craft" he said. "They know just when it is coming. See how they head for the middle of the river, where the Bore is at its lowest."

He was right. Small tugs, launches and those practically circular wherries peculiar to the Hooghly were all lying in mid river, well away from either Bank. An eerie silence fell. The whole world waited.

A muted roar came faintly from downstream. A cross between an express train and the boom of surf on a beach.

"Stand well clear of the bollards" called the Berthing Master.

Round the far bend came a wall of water, leaping through the rushes and small trees on the bank. Foaming and falling, splashing and swirling, clearly visible in the starlight. It must have been moving at six or seven knots. Somewhere a tug began a frantic hooting, warning her companions of the imminent approach of the Bore. I looked over side. The river was still running out at three knots. The ship was still riding to her bow moorings. The cargo pumps had been stopped, in case the flexible hoses burst.

There came a tremendous cracking sound from the poop as the after moorings suddenly got the full weight of the ship surging forward on the crest of the Bore.

In the space of half a minute, a twelve thousand ton tanker was lifted two feet and left riding to a four knot flood tide, where before she had ridden to a three knot ebb. Meanwhile the Bore its crest flecked with mud, broken branches and other rubbish, raced off into the dark, leaving San Vito ranging up and down, her chains cracking with the strain, before settling to her stern mooring. Within twenty minutes of the Bore's coming and going she was discharging cargo again. The small craft had vanished into the night and all was back to normal.

I went aft to examine the moorings, for I wanted to see for myself what they were like. The heavy links of the anchor cables had bitten deep into the steel of the bollards and some of the links

A typical Eagle Line tanker, The *San Emiliano*.

were jammed. They would take some shifting when it came to un-mooring. At least, I thought, our hard work had not been in vain, the moorings had held.

On a later occasion our Berthing Master was killed at Buj-Buj. An American T.2. had been discharging cargo and her Captain refused to stop pumping for the Bore. Some of her after moorings had parted and the pipeline pontoon had ridden under the main pontoon, causing the hose to burst under the tremendous pressure. A jet of petrol had struck a lamp standard, fusing the light and igniting the petrol. In seconds the jetty was ablaze. The Berthing Master and four coolies had jumped into the river, their clothing ablaze. They were not seen again. The swift undercurrents of the Hooghly had dragged them to their doom.

Calcutta was a wonderful, colourful city. Its many fine buildings contrasted with, in the back streets, some of the most dreadful slums. It was full of troops, being a transit camp and leave centre for the Fourteenth Army, then engaged with the Japanese in Burma.

Roy, the 2nd Mate, and I strolled up Chowringhee and across the Maidan, drinking in the sights and smells of this proud and ancient city. Founded by Clive.

I was struck by two things. The ancient 1928 vintage taxis. These tore through the streets, bulb horn blaring, the beards and turbans of the driver and his mate streaming in the breeze. Such men as these would ride the plains of India in another age. Ghenghis Khan in modern garb.

The second thing was the inordinate numbers of lovely women who were to be seen on the arms of Army lieutenants and RAF pilot officers, fresh from the fighting. Where, we wondered, did such beauties come from? No service officer could have his wife with him in war time India. Closer examination revealed the answer.

"Say, Steve, have you noticed something about these girls?"

"No, can't say I have"

"They're all Chi-chi women" said Roy. And so they were. Anglo-Indian lovelies.

We never tried to get off with any of them. Somehow, I didn't think a civilian sailorman could compete with Subalterns and glamour boys.

The train which ran between Calcutta and Buj-Buj was a combination of Heath Robinson and British Railways. Composed of three venerable six-wheeled coaches and an ancient high funnelled tank engine, it ran more or less regularly. The coaches had no windows, only wooden Jalousies, long since splintered and broken to matchwood. This left the compartments open to the elements, and the occupants to the wide eyed and curious gaze of the multitude. Leaving Buj-Buj we sat in a first class compartment. This was distinguished from third class by moth-eaten and flea ridden upholstery. The train stopped at several small stations as well as one or two unscheduled places. At each stop, more and more Dhoti clad bodies piled on board, till it was impossible to get any more inside. This did not deter those who were left. They clung to the footboards, and sat between the coaches on the couplings. From the sounds over our heads it was evident that the more agile had even perched themselves up there. The noise and smell were indescribable.

Malaria was rife up the Hooghly. Once darkness fell myriads of mosquitoes descended upon the ship, making life a misery. We became covered with painful, itchy lumps. We were of course on anti-malarial pills. The only remedy was to smear citronella oil on our skins and bury ourselves under a mosquito net. I bought one in Calcutta and rigged it up in my cabin over my bunk. Its folds were stifling in such a sticky climate, but it was that or be bitten to death. The anti-malarial we were using was Mepacrine, which had the effect of turning the skin yellow. *San Vito's* crew looked like a bunch of Chinamen.

On 5th March we departed thankfully from Buj-Buj, once more in the care of a Bengal Pilot. This time he had a young Indian apprentice with him. Captain Smith asked how the lad was doing.

"Gad sir! These wallahs will never make pilots on this river"

He kept the lad in the chains, swinging the lead for hours.

"Teach him to learn the river properly" was his comment.

Somehow I felt that studying a chart would have had a better effect on the boy's knowledge.

From Buj-Buj we returned to Abadan, arriving at "our" jetty on 21st March. We had now been away from home nine months, six of which had been spent in the Indian Ocean and Persian Gulf. We were tired, and oh, Brother! we were bored. I looked out of my cabin port at the tall columns of the cracking towers, at the silver chimneys of that power house – at the heat, the dust, the awful flatness of the desert and the river.

Somewhere in the accommodation I heard a great yell of joy. Huh! Someone must be pleased with life. Bully for him.

Came the sound of running feet. The Second Mate burst in through the door, grabbed me and started waltzing round the room.

"Drydock! Drydock! Wonderful beautiful Drydock" he chanted.

"When?" I asked. My spirits were slow to rise.

"Now! This time. Bombay. Have you heard? OH BOY! Just let me get my feet ashore in a civilised place. Whoopee!"

"Have you thought what it means?" I asked.

"Sure" he said. "It means shore! All those lovely Chi-Chi girls"

"It means" I said heavily, "That this bloody ship is never going to go home. If we drydock out here we'll do another nine months out East. And what's so cheerful about that?"

"Aw! Come on Steve boy. Cheer up. Think of all those gorgeous gals in Poona. Think of all the lovely ice cold beer there is in Bombay"

In spite of my gloom, the Second Mate's infectious high spirits had their effect.

"Let's celebrate" I said. "I've been keeping a bottle for this occasion. Get the glasses".

We drank to Bombay in warm, treacly Guinness.

6

NEARING THE END

On Friday, 30th March, 1945, *San Vito* berthed at Pir Pau, the Shell Company's oil terminal in Bombay. Some seven miles from the city, the jetty to which the ship was moored was reached over mud flats by a rickety wooden pier some quarter of a mile long. That first evening I took a walk to the shore to stretch my legs. Standing in the mud, thigh deep, were several Indians. I stopped to watch, intrigued.

A man would slowly lift one leg and push it into the glittering mud, groping with his toes. Straightening out his leg he would pull it clear to reveal a silver fish about the size of a sardine, clamped between his toes. The fish lived deep in the mud and the natives had devised this ingenious way of catching them. What a way to earn a living.

Bombay is built on a peninsula and the magnificent harbour is on the Eastern side of this finger of land. The Western side is known as Back Bay and contains a wonderful Lido called Breach Kandy. At this time it was used by the hundreds of troops then stationed in Bombay. We used it well.

The cargo supervisor was a young Indian called Tipnis. We found him very agreeable and polite, and helped him all we could. To repay what he insisted was our kindness he invited the three Mates, rather diffidently to his home, once the ship had docked.

We lay out in the bay, cleaning tanks for several days. Around us lay various rusty, burnt out wrecks, victims of the "Bombay Explosion" which had devastated the harbour some months before.

The tank cleaning was done by a cheerful crew, something that had not been seen on board for many weeks. The prospect of a break ashore put the lads in high spirits.

On 5th April, *San Vito* hove up and slowly approached the entrance locks of the harbour proper. Within two hours she was resting gratefully on the blocks of Mazagon Drydock. The shores were in and she would be there for several weeks.

Though there was lots for the officers to attend to during the day, evenings and weekends were free.

We made the most of our spare time, after such a spell of hard running as we had done recently.

On our first evening Roy and I decided to have a stroll up town. We passed through the famous Gateway to India, erected in honour of Queen Victoria. It reminded me of Marble Arch. Before us was the great ornate pile of the Taj Mahal Hotel, one of the biggest in Bombay.

"Well, we may as well start here" said Roy.

We crossed the road, narrowly missing being run down by a flying taxi and entered the foyer of this famous and sumptuous hotel. Great chandeliers hung from gilded ceilings. The furnishings, both hard and soft, were in gold and red. Punka fans swished noiselessly to keep the air circulating.

We moved to the lounge and were served drinks by an attentive bearer. Under the discreet lighting beautifully gowned ladies and their immaculate escorts stood in little groups, or sat around. Somewhere a radio dispensed soft dance music.

"What price the *Vito* now?" I asked Roy, as we sipped ice cold beer.

Roy was looking about him with a grin of satisfaction. I followed his gaze to where three young women had just entered and sat down near us. Unattached girls in a place like this?

"Come on" I said "Let's go".

"OK" said Roy. He sounded doubtful. "But I bet they're waiting for someone".

"Maybe for us" I murmured hopefully. "Let's have a go, anyway".

"May we join you?" I asked politely.

"You may" said one. "But we are waiting for someone".

The voice, the tone, was glacial.

We tried to make conversation with these girls, but were handed the frozen mitt at every turn. They just did not want to know us. The conversation had died a natural death. We were about to take our leave, when,

"Darling, how lovely to see you"

I turned to see three Naval Officers, loaded to the gunwales with gold braid, bearing down on our table.

"Come on" said Roy. "No room for you and I in this lot"

The girls did not even see us go. This was typical of the whole of India in the last war. Pretty young women with white skins were really at a premium. Those who did go to India went as Wrens, ATS and Forces girls of one kind or another. They were in great demand, so much so that no ordinary ranker or civilian could get a look in. Even if a girl fell for a soldier, where could he take her? The hotels and decent restaurants were out of bounds to Other Ranks. All the squaddie had to offer his girl was the NAAFI, the YMCA or the TOC H. No girl could be expected to go to these places and be stared at, whistled at, or even fought over, by men lonely for the company of the opposite sex. So the officers were the ones who cashed in. Service girls were allowed to go out in evening dress and who was to say anything to a pretty private dancing with the C.O? It was a most unfair system. Far better if none of the Women's Services had been allowed in India.

Next day was Sunday. On our arrival in Bombay some of the officers had been measured for tropical suits. These had been made and delivered to the ship on her dry-docking. Not bad going.

This was the day we were due to visit Mr Tipnis. After lunch John Gay, Roy Bowlerwell and I hailed a taxi outside Red Gate. We gave him the name of the street Tipnis had mentioned.

"Atcha, Sahib" said the bearded Sikh driver.

Down went his foot to the floorboards and we shot through the crowded streets. The car was an Invicta open tourer of 1928 vintage, but he drove it like a Ferrari. Pedestrians, rickshaws, gharries, scattered like corn in the whirlwind of our passage.

"Lord!" prayed the Mate. "Don't let 'im hit anybody, or we'll be torn limb from limb by the multitude"

Now we had left the centre of town far behind and were some-where in the Northwest suburbs of Bombay. The streets teemed with white dhoti-clad Indians, their wives dressed in gaily coloured saris. There was not a white face anywhere to be seen. In about twenty minutes the driver pulled over a corner.

"Ten rupees, Sahib" he said before we could ask the fare.

John paid up, gave him one extra for luck. With his standard of driving he'd need it.

Out of the throng came Mr Tipnis, dressed in white shirt and trousers. He wore a tie. We suddenly felt overdressed.

"Good afternoon, gentlemen. You found the place all right?"

He led us down a side street then into another. We came to a small square of villas, each in its own grounds. An oasis in the hubbub of the city.

"I didn't realise it could be so peaceful only minutes from the main road" I said.

Tipnis smiled as he opened the big green gates leading into the approach.

"From my window I can see the sea."

The house was square, with two floors, each surrounded by a wide shaded veranda. With its wide arched doorways and big, jalousied windows, it was a cool haven in the dusty heat of the afternoon. We went into a large hallway, tiled in green, through which soughed a cool breeze. Tipnis struck a little brass gong. From a doorway came a young Indian woman dressed in a primrose sari. She was rather plump, her black oiled hair sleek about her head. On her wide brows the red mark denoting her married state had been freshly painted.

"Gentlemen may I present my wife?"

Gracefully the lady placed her two hands together, palms touching and bowed to each of us in turn. Then she withdrew.

Through another door Tipnis led us into a cool, high ceilinged room, sparsely furnished with rattan chairs and tables. This room, like the hall, was also tiled halfway up in green and cream. On the floor which was of wood, was a beautiful Indian carpet, surrounded by smaller Persian Bokhara prayer rugs.

A tall, white haired Indian rose to greet us.

"May I present my father?" said Tipnis.

With dignity, yet with a delightful informality, Tipnis senior accepted the introductions.

"Won't you sit down gentlemen? My son has had lots to tell me regarding your kindness to him".

We sat and talked for about an hour. We were offered refreshing lemon tea, served by a maidservant. There was no alcohol. It would have been out of place in that house.

Our conversation ranged over a wide variety of subjects. The progress of the war, Indian and British history, education and politics. Our rather rusty brains were bemused by the erudition of the Tipnis father and son. But at no time were we made to feel that the British Raj was unwelcome in India.

From somewhere in the house came the faint sound of a gong.

"Ah dinner at last" said Mr. Tipnis, senior.

He led the way across the hall to a room, whose coolness was even more marked than the one we had left. Round the table, set for five places, stood three Indian ladies. As we entered, each inclined her head and pressed her palms together. One of the ladies was Mrs. Tipnis, the others I later discovered were Tipnis's younger sisters.

These two graceful young women came round the table to each of us. One carried a brass bowl and a flask of water, and washed our hands. The other carried soap and a towel, with which she helped her sister and afterwards dried our hands.

Then came dinner. I am very fond of curry, but this was a dream of a meal. Served with poppadams and small chupattis, it had a fire which did not burn the mouth, but left only the flavour. Afterwards there was tea, and a dish of honey sweet cakes, rather like petit fours.

We strolled upstairs to the veranda on the West side of the villa. Young Tipnis dispensed Burma cheroots of exceptionally fine quality – a far cry from the kind I was normally able to buy.

"We always watch the sunset on Sunday evenings" he said "It's the only evening on which we can relax properly".

Across the roof tops, already in shadow, the red ball of the sun plunged down for the horizon through a tracery of palm leaves. So hot did it look that we almost expected to hear it hiss as its lower limb cut the blue of the ocean. Overhead golden Alto-Cumulus slowly turned to pink fire, to deep crimson and finally to the purple glow that so often is the brief twilight of the Tropics. As darkness rolled up from the East, the city became a blaze of twinkling lights.

At 9 p.m. we rose to say thanks and farewell to the ladies.

"I shall walk you to the street, where you will find a taxi" volunteered Tipnis Junior.

We soon discovered why he had offered to come with us. The streets so confused and crowded by day, were doubly so in the dark. Naphtha flare lamps roared and hissed perilously close to bales of cotton and other flimsy goods. People jostled and crowded past. I had to pick my way among sleeping bodies, lying all over the pavements and gutters. These are the homeless of India. All they possess, if they are lucky, is a string bed, on which they can lie in the street at night.

"Safer to walk in the centre of the road" suggested Tipnis.

We passed a garishly lit archway.

"Dr. Chandirams Celebrated Waxworks" said the sign over the door.

"Can we go and have a look?" I asked.

"Certainly" said Tipnis "It is a very good show".

It cost half a rupee to go in, to find ourselves in another world. Discreetly illuminated, the goddess Siva stared over our heads, her several arms radiating about her like sunbeams.

There were several alcoves. In each was a scene from Hindu mythology. A holy man, seated on a bed of nails while a pretty girl advanced and retreated from round a corner of the cave. Each time she appeared his head turned towards her.

"He can only renounce the world of the flesh when he has ceased to gaze on her beauty" whispered Tipnis.

We went round the other scenes, Tipnis explaining in his soft Indian voice the significance of each one. We returned to the brashness of the outside world. It had been a good eight annas worth.

The rest of the week was spent working hard on the ship, during the day, and seeing the sights of Bombay at night. There were plenty of good cinemas. There was an E.N.S.A. theatre where I saw Dame Edith Evans and Jane Hylton. Breach Kandy was a favourite swimming place, and duties were arranged so that the junior officers could go there on alternate afternoons.

But during the week, something occurred which thrilled the younger officers of *SanVito* and even caused the older and wiser to

rouse themselves into a cheerful frame of mind. Captain Smith
started it. He came back from the Burma-Shell office on Wednesday,
with an invitation from the Storage and Export Manager and his
wife, to a dinner dance in the Ritz Hotel on Friday. This was extended
to all the ship's officers, Deck, Engineer and Radio. Apparently, as
part of their war effort, the Export Manager asked the various ladies
of the Shell Staff, and the wives and daughters of employees, if
they would act as hostesses to the officer personnel of any ship of
the Shell Group, which happened to be in port, at a function once
a month. Since *San Vito* was the only "Shell" tanker in Bombay, it
was our good fortune to be chosen.

Out of sixteen officers on board the ship all but four were able
to attend. Friday found the accommodation of *Vito* a madhouse of
mates and engineers ironing their Number Tens, or rushing round
borrowing vital pieces of equipment.

"Dick,. can you loan me a collar stud?"

"Does my white jacket fit?"

"Hell's bells. A hole in my sock. My only bloody pair".

"That's all right, Mate, Blanco your heel and it won't show!"

By dint of much swopping, safety pinning and swearing, a round
dozen of us finally stood ready and waiting, a good half hour before
the promised transport was due. The evening was a lovely, cool
one, with an early moon showing over the harbour. A bit of joshing
and kidding went on, but underneath every one was a little keyed
up. None of us wanted to let down the good name of the company.
This sounds priggish, but there was a certain professional jealousy
between Shell and Eagle ships.

"Here comes the jitney" someone called, and round the corner
of the pumphouse came a little lorry. It was a conversion of an
Austin Sixteen. The body had been removed and a bus like contraption with two rows of seats fitted in its place. In a moment the
jitney was rolling out of the Red Gate, full of excited young men.
It was no time before it pulled up outside the magnificent facade
of the Ritz. The Taj Mahal is a fine hotel but the Ritz beats it hollow.
As we eagerly de-bussed, the strains of a dance band and the muted
hum of conversation came from inside.

Our host and his wife, Mr. and Mrs. Stevens, met us in the foyer.

Soon we were drinking cocktails and being introduced to our gorgeous dancing partners. As each girl arrived she was surrounded by twelve eager officers, and plied with cigarettes, lights and drinks. She was asked her name. Mrs. Stevens, who had obviously planned a more formal introduction, stood apprehensively by the side of her grinning husband, who was enjoying the situation.

After one or two drinks, and when there were no more girls due to arrive, Mrs Stevens entered the dining room on the arm of First Officer John Gay. The rest of us followed, an excited animated group of young people, out to enjoy ourselves. Now came a problem. Only eight girls had turned up. To distribute nine ladies and thirteen men evenly around a dining table would seem to be difficult. But it worked out admirably, for the simple reason that no girl was at the table for more than a few minutes. As soon as the band struck up, all the girls were whisked on to the floor. The faces of the waiters grew steadily longer as their excellent soup, fish and meat courses were removed virtually untouched. The gravy on the chicken congealed. The ice cream melted. The crew of *SanVito* danced on, uncaring. All I recall having to eat was two spoonfuls of soup and a Brussels sprout.

As for the girls, they thought we were wonderful. After several drinks we were full of wit. We were all keen dancers, inspired by our captivating partners. To us they were delightful, creatures of another world. A world more civilised, more normal, more peaceful. They reminded us of home, of our own kind. We danced them off their pretty little feet. In no time it was Midnight and time for us to leave.

Regretfully we saw them into the cars which came for them, before returning to the ship. Conversation was excited on the way back.

"That Sylvia, now. She was a stunner"

"I don't know. I liked Judith. So young" This from the young cadet.

"Haw! Haw!" A guffaw of laughter shook the jitney "What makes you think you're so mature".

We chattered on, comparing notes. We found that each and every girl had been asked at some time during the evening, for a date by each and every boy. And each and every girl had said no.

It must have been a conspiracy.

That we had made a hit with the ladies of Shell was made clear the following day. On behalf of the ship's officers, the Mate sent the cadet and a Junior Engineer up to the office with a huge bouquet of flowers for Mrs. Stevens, who was in charge of the typing pool. The boys returned after lunch and reported a most successful mission. The sight of two good looking ship's officers in the typing pool had caused something of a sensation. One or two of the girls of the previous evening worked in the pool and introduced Arthur and Bill to the rest of the girls. One of the latter, a ravishing redhead, had invited the Officers of *San Vito* to the Indian Army Service Club that evening. Her father was the C.O. and she assured the boys that he would be pleased to welcome us.

An air of excitement pervaded *San Vito* that afternoon. Our combined wardrobe of whites was pooled once again, to enable those who were off duty to go to the Club.

At eight p.m. six of us piled into a taxi outside the docks and headed for Kolaba Causeway, where the Club was situated. This is a residential district to the south of Bombay. On each side of the wide boulevard were lovely big houses. One of these was the club. Katherine, the redhead met us, and tripped gaily up the stair to the dance floor. As we followed Katherine across the tiled floor, all eyes were on us. The place was full of Army Officers and we noticed one or two N.C.O.'s.

Katherine's father, Captain Van Haiften, was of Dutch extraction. A tall, lean, leathery man of great charm and kindliness. He introduced us to his wife, a plump, motherly lady, whose dark colour was obvious.

The Mate was talking quietly in my ear.

"Steve – looks as if we've landed among the Chi-Chis".

So it proved. We had met up with a part of that community which had grown inevitably, out of the years of British rule in India, the Anglo-Indians. This group of mixed blood reached far back in time, to the days of Clive and the French. Yet they always tried to out-British the British. Their English was impeccable. It had a curiously clipped and sing-song intonation, which once heard, remained in the memory, and wherever heard thereafter, stamped "Chi-Chi" on the speaker. Their way of life was as English as they could make it. They even referred to England as "Home" though none of them had ever seen it. Shunned by the Indians, despised by the British, they had made a world of living, peculiar to themselves. They did jobs of the half world. Jobs which were beyond most Indians, yet considered to be too menial by the British in India. They ran the railways, most efficiently. Right from the top down to the drivers and firemen, signal men and permanent way inspectors. Their handsome, virile sons filled the lower executive jobs in commerce and industry. Their daughters, glorious creatures, combining the best features of Indian and English, worked as hotel receptionists, typists, stenographers and shop assistants in the big stores of the cities.

We found Anglo-Indians extremely kind and agreeable. They could not do enough for us. If I want to be cynical, I could say this was because they hoped their daughters might marry a white man. This may well have been the case, but in contrast to the snooty indifference of the British residents in India, the Anglo-Indians were most friendly and hospitable to we men of the sea, who had paused but briefly on their shores. If they hoped that their lovely and attractive daughters might hook one of us, they never gave the slightest sign, by word or deed, that this was so. I remember them with gratitude and affectionate pity. How they fare in the new India I have no knowledge. I wish them well. For the mingling of Indian and English blood, produced a very good type of human being. Excitable, passionate, yet with a loyalty to duty and friends that was impressive.

It has been said that Eurasian girls are gorgeous up to the age of twenty five. After that they "go to seed". Some do, I suppose. But if Mrs. Van Haiften was an example, certainly she had grown plump. She was about forty, a gracious and cultured woman and the essence of hospitality. Her home was a real home for her four beautiful daughters and two handsome sons. There was no doubt that Van Haiften worshipped her. He called her Mother. And that's what she was, in the best sense of the word.

To return to the dance. It was again an unqualified success. Since we were all keen dancers we did not lack for partners.

I found myself dancing several times with a slim raven haired creature. She was feather light in my arms. Her name was Lenore. The perfume of her sleek, shining hair against my cheek was disturbing. To counter her effect on me I asked,

"How about telling me who everyone is at our table?"

I led her back to the table where our party had been watching us dance. A little ripple of applause broke as we sat down.

"You dance very well together" said Mrs. Van Haiften.

Everyone resumed talking and Lenore set about telling me who our party was. Her voice was silver music in my ears. She was a very attractive young lady. Finally I asked

"And who is the little dark girl right opposite us? Your sister?"

Lenore laughed delightedly, clapping her hands to her face.

"Oh David. You are funny That's Mummy. I must tell her"

She ran round the table to speak to the lady, who smiled and beckoned to me. I went over, feeling a bit foolish.

"Where did you learn to compliment a lady so charmingly?" Lenore's Mother asked teasingly.

I mumbled something.

"Now you must dance with Mummy" said Lenore.

Her mother, too, was a lovely dancer. She told me that her husband, an engineer, spent long periods away from home. At present he was in Calcutta. She was poised, assured, and altogether charming.

The dance ended at midnight. Mrs. Van Haiften who had captivated the Mate, called out, after the National Anthem,

"Everybody comes back home for supper"

San Vito's officers had attached themselves to one or other of the girls. I found Lenore.

"Will you come with me?" I asked "I'll find a taxi" She looked doubtful for a moment.

"Just a tick, I'll go and see Mummy". She was back in a flash.

"Mummy says it's OK. But we must not spend your money on a taxi. We'll walk from here. It's not far".

We left the lights and sounds of the Club behind and set off, hand in hand down the moonlit boulevard. Beyond the houses we could hear the boom of the surf on the beach, and glimpse it through gaps in the trees.

Was this really happening! I asked myself. Only days before I
had been on the high seas, where women like Lenore were impossible, hopeless dreams. Now I was walking entranced beside a lovely
girl. I glanced down at her. I am not tall, yet she reached barely to
the shoulder of my jacket. In her white dance frock, given an
emerald sheen by the moonglow, its light glinting highlights in
her raven hair, her eyes dark and sparkling with excitement, she
was an enchanting vision of loveliness, caught in a moment of
time.

We stopped beneath the dark shadow of a mango tree. Fireflies
darted about us. The distant hum of the city was drowned in the
shrill chirping of crickets.

"Let's go David" she whispered. "Else the others will be wondering where we are".

During the rest of our stay in Bombay the Van Haiften's large
and rambling house became our home. At any time of the day or
evening we were free to call. To go for a swim from their private
beach at the bottom of the garden. To help little Tommy with his
model plane. To wash up the dishes. To play records and dance. Or
simply to sit round in a friendly atmosphere and talk.

The eldest daughter June was nineteen. She was married to a
British N.C.O. and they had a young baby. Their happiness was
lovely to see, but I wondered, what happens when the war is over?
In a new India would there be room for white Bruce and his lovely,
titian haired June?

After four weeks *San Vito* was nearly ready for sea. Even the
hospitality of the Van Haiften family had begun to pall. Most of us
were running short of rupees and, God help us, we were beginning
to wish we were back at sea.

It is a strange fact that the human mind will only retain in
memory the better aspects of a particular situation or period of
time. No matter how ghastly the experience, or how long it lasted,
the mind will recall only the highlights, the funny side, or the
friendships made in adversity. I have spoken to friends held captive
by the enemy and their recollections, while blasphemous in regard
to their guards, and the food, were in the main humorous. They
retained only the lighter side of their life behind the wire. Never

the sense of desperate boredom, never the hardships or the pains of hunger in their bellies, never the actual smell of fear. It is perhaps as well that this is so, for in this way life, particularly at sea, can be made bearable.

(Keats) "Poetry is emotion recollected in tranquillity". So it is with the sailor. Seafaring is remembered in the sailor's mind by the funny thing which happened to him in Madras, or London, or Lagos, or 'Frisco. His memory, unless he keeps a journal, becomes fragmentary and as it does so, the hardships and disappointments fade.

My friendship with Lenore had hit a sticky patch. She was still sweet, and I felt that she was waiting for something further from me. Yet I held back. I was too much of a coward to examine closely how I felt for Lenore.

John Gay caught me in my cabin one day. I was busy dressing to go ashore.

"I want a word with you, young Steve".

"OK Fire ahead. But I am in a hurry" I adjusted my tie.

"What are your intentions with regard to Lenore?"

I paused, the hair brushes in my hands.

"What do you mean, John?"

"You know very well what I mean. That girl thinks you intend to marry her. She thinks you are too shy to ask her".

"Get away man! It's only a bit of fun. I'm engaged back home".

"Is it?" the Mate's voice was serious. He leaned forward.

"Look lad. These people have been more than good to us. They are the salt of the earth. But" he paused, then went on "What would your parents say if you took them a Chi-Chi bride?"

"Don't talk nonsense" I retorted angrily.

John shrugged his shoulders.

"OK It's none of my business. But – have you told Lenore you have a girl back home?"

"No" I muttered.

"Well just think about it lad. Think about it".

I did think about it. All the way out of the docks and through the streets of Bombay. Surely I hadn't given Lenore reason to think I was serious. A bit of kissing and cuddling. A few evenings at a romantic restaurant, the Argentine. A few more in her flat, while Mother was at the cinema. Could she make this into a picture of serious courtship? I was forced to admit that she could. The question now was, did I really want her for my wife?

I shook my head as if to clear it. No of course not. I thought of the cold dampness of England. Lenore was like a lovely orchid, perfect in the hot house of India. In England she might wither and die.

She was very composed when I told her Goodbye.

The following morning *San Vito* moved into the waiting berth for the locks. At last we were outward bound.

A big trooper was coming in through the locks. She was the *Monarch of Bermuda* a 20,000 ton liner of Furness Withy. The Indians who handled the warping wires on the lock walls were experts. One would hold his wire round the electric capstan till it hummed and whipped the air under the strain, only to release it at the very moment of breaking. He would then hurry along to the next capstan as the ship moved slowly through.

Then it was our turn. In no time we were dropping the pilot off Kolaba Point. I tried to make out Van Haiften's house, but it was obscured by trees. They had all come earlier to wave us "Au Revoir". Neither Lenore or her Mother were there. *SanVito's* whistle sounded the three long blasts of farewell. It was forbidden in wartime, but just this once, Captain Smith agreed to it.

7
BEGINNING TO WIN

Homeward Bound, via Malacca Straits and Singapore. After our dry dock in Bombay lasting a few weeks during which all the officers and engineers of *San Vito* had a really wonderful time. For the first time in ten long weary months they could relax away from war danger in a city which still hummed with all the vigour and bustle of Indian life under the last days of the Raj.

From Bombay we sailed for Colombo in Ceylon. Captain Smith returned from Naval Control Office with orders to go round the coast to the very large Combined Operations Bay of Trincomalee.

In the beautiful bay, full of the build up of an invasion task force, we were requisitioned by Admiralty as an M.F.A – never heard of before we became "Merchant Fleet Auxiliary" one of the very few taken up for this forthcoming invasion, though we knew nothing of where it would take place. We sailed, bound for Aden, back across the Indian Ocean. On arrival in Aden six five-hundred ton barges full of fresh water came alongside but our tanks were not fit to accept water. Within hours an army of coolies, paid at one rupee per day descended and cement washed Nos. 1 to 5 cargo tanks ready to accept five thousand tons of water. Cargo tanks numbers 6, 7 and 8 were loaded with marine diesel oil. We took the fresh water across the Gulf of Aden to Djibouti, and the diesel to Port Sudan, thence all the way to Trincomalee via Aden where we loaded 5000 tons of diesel. But on the way we diverted to Vizagapatam on the East Coast of India. This was a small port where we had to load 5000 tons of water through ordinary fire hoses "over the top" into the open tank lid covers. It took a week, during which we had a cyclone over thirty six hours. At its height we started to break our ten inch mooring, re-splicing ropes and wires, till the storm moved on, leaving two cargo vessels ashore outside the harbour. Later in the day a 7000 ton liberty ship limped into port, her funnel dented and streaked with salt spray and two damaged life boats.

From Vizagapatam back to Trincomalee where we took on over a hundred 40 gallon lub-oil drums, several tons of potatoes, and food rations, cigarettes and sweets, plus other odds and ends, all on deck for the troops. We still had no idea except our M.F.A. title was used by the naval authority. Under the usual brown envelope "orders" we set off eastwards this time under "most secret" orders. We followed instructions as prescribed and one day realised we were heading for the Nicobar Islands.

One day I was completing my noon sight when the lookout shouted "mine dead ahead". I dashed from chart room to spot the mine, its horns seeming to loom large and ominous. "Hard – a – Starboard" for moments as the mine headed for the bow wave on the port side. "Hard to Port" was my final order to swing the stern clear as the mine passed down shipside some twenty feet clear. It was a "Zigzag".

Our secret orders were positions of latitude and longitude which gave us our navigation from say Point AB to Point AC.

Our next position was in a bay of Nicobar Islands which we approached carefully in a tremendous downpour of rain. We rounded a point and there, spread before us was what we thought was the Japanese Navy.

Two large battleships, two impressive aircraft carriers, and the usual miscellany of smaller vessels. "It's our own navy" shouted the look out. "Its the Nelson". The unusual configuration of the ship which had three sixteen inch gun turrets forward of her massive bridge structure and one on her after deck reassured us. Nelson originally was designed with two turrets forward and two aft and weigh 45,000 tons. But Britain and Germany agreed in the late twenties to a limit of 35,000 tons. Hitler's Bismarck and Tirpitz ended up as 41,700 tons and Britain with Renown at 30,700 and Nelson, shortened by a few hundred feet to reduce her to a three turret ship and 36,000 tons in 1939.

Our orders were to anchor in the "fleet" supply anchorage in a tightly arranged row of supply ships of all kinds, of which we were the sole merchant tanker. Beside *Nelson* lay HMS *Nigeria*, a 10,000 ton member of the Colony class cruisers.

Later in 1957 when I was senior pilot Takoradi, Ghana I piloted *Nigeria* into Takoradi, being at 555 feet long, one of the longest to "swing" off her berth.

Three days later we were sent to Penang. Its capital is the most lovely Georgetown at the head of Malacca Straits. Twenty four hours later we were shepherded out of the bay under the care of two trawler minesweepers who guided us down the swept channel. No other traffic was seen and about two days later one trawler stopped sweeping and came alongside to give us another envelope of orders and told us to steer course 085 degrees to take part in an invasion operation.

In the distance we could hear a bombardment. Malaya appeared to us as a low lying area some miles south of Port Dickson and known as Port Swettenham. Later this landing was called Morib Beachhead. As we neared the shore a great convoy of vessels appeared. The Headquarters ship called HMS *Glenroy* an extremely modern merchant ship of Shire Line whose signal lamps flashed continuously to everyone and was able to direct us into a "supply" anchorage. Our old friends from Nicobar Islands lay a quarter of a mile from us. *Nelson, Nigeria, Hunter* – (an Escort carrier) destroyers and loading craft of all kinds, all known by initials LCI(P) LCQ LCR LCT LST.

We lay abandoned as it were for three days. Captain Smith was becoming very worried – no one wanted to know us. Finally we lowered a boat and I went with him as escort officer to visit *Glenroy* for orders.

HMS *Glenroy* under the white Ensign was very "pusser" Her accommodation gangway was spotless and all brass polished. We saluted as we went on deck and listened to the "pipe the side" greeting. The officer of the day spoke into an intercom and led Captain Smith away into the bowels of the ship while I was left on deck under the basilisk stare of the second OOD.

Half an hour later the master returned and we were piped overside into our lifeboat and back to *San Vito* "to await orders" was all Captain Smith told us.

So we waited for four more days and learned a lot of news from the small craft which started to take water and small stores from us. The initial landing had been somewhat of a failure. The 4000 ton landing ship tanks LST had grounded on a sand bank some twenty yards from the shore, so the tank rolled off the bowramp and disappeared up to tank hatch level. The smaller landing craft tanks – LCTs were able to land their three tanks because they could get closer to the beach while the larger LSTs grounded on the sand bank. All the LCMS, LCPs, LCQs could land their marines and soldiers happily on the beach, ready to fight a non-existent Japanese army which had withdrawn. Imagine a vast invasion force now having to be re-embarked. What a job to do.

So many of the smaller invasion craft but including the big 4000 ton tank landing ships started to call for water and diesel fuel. The ship lay to her anchor in a 2 knot tide flow and we found the old lady being nudged up her bottom so to speak.. Most vessels approached from behind and six out of ten were carried by wind or tide under the stern quarter, sometimes bumping to leave a small dent.

We decided to paint a large black square on the ships port side amidships as a target, the best side for vessels to come alongside due to wind and tide. In 15 inch white painted legend read "AIM HERE".

One morning a little Chris Craft LC1(P) came alongside and hailed O.O.W.

"Have you any water to spare?"

"Come aboard" was the reply, "We've got 5000 tons to get rid of".

Three marines climbed our short boarding ladder with 2 jerricans each. This was their total water capacity for the boat. 6 x 8 – 48 gallons.

Their food supply also was meagre. Mostly tinned "iron rations" – no fresh food. They told us the only way they got a good nights rest was to go up one of the innumerable creeks for about a mile and tie up to the bank to be eaten alive by mosquitoes.

"D'you really have 5000 tons of water?" asked the corporal.

So we showed him the open tank lid of No 3 Centre full to the brim with 550 tons of clean pure water.

As the three soldiers left an hour or so later loaded with their water and cigarettes from our naval stocks – signed for 5 times! they asked

"Can we tell the others?"

"Sure" said our chief officer, that's what we're here for.".

We soon realised that we needed hoses of small bore to fill the tanks of LCMs, LC1s and such receptacles as jerricans. Tommy Robson our chief engineer had the solution. Fitting a "reducing piece" from our 8" discharge pipe lines to the admiralty 5" and adapting a blank face into which were screwed our 1 1/2" steaming cleaning hoses, they were excellent water hosepipes, with the advantage that they could be screwed together to make a hose as long as might be.

After Singapore we returned to Trincomalee, with some 2000 tons of fresh water and 1600 tons of marine diesel (gas oil). In Trincomalee the naval authority now that Japan had surrendered and peace was at hand, were not interested in what we had left in the ship. We were de-requisitioned and told to proceed to Colombo for orders. The afternoon before we sailed a small fleet naval tanker came alongside and asked to top up his tanks. Thankfully we got rid of 1000 tons of gas oil and some water, and the remaining drums of lub oil on deck.

Halfway back across the Indian Ocean, we got a message from Radio Bombay San Vito proceed Abadan to load. So once again our bows headed up the Gulf of Oman, round the Quoin Islands and into the Persian Gulf. An air of gloom pervaded the ship. How many more times would we navigate the muddy waters of the Shatt-al-Arab River, only to load yet again for somewhere East of Suez.

We steamed up the last 11 miles of the Shatt River for Kabda to Abadan under a sky of grey clouds in the last weeks of November 1945.

This far north up the Gulf in winter it was cold, around 55 degrees F dropping to 35 degrees in the night. Expecting to anchor in Bawards Reach below the oil berths, we were surprised to find our favourite berthing pilot Captain Dick Scott had come to berth us at our normal berth No.22. He had some good news for us "I hear you're to load for the UK this time". The news flashed through the ship like wild fire and by the time we docked the atmosphere aboard was full of joyous anticipation. The spell of "East of Suez" was to be broken at last.

We tried to work out that the ship would get home for Christmas and if all went well we could do it with days to spare.

Just as were due to sail Roy, our 2nd officer, had the most atrocious stroke of bad luck. He was exchanged with one of our other Second Officers from one of our ships which had landed him in Abadan two weeks previously. Roy, whose wife had had a baby a few months previously was really cross about the transfer, and was only mollified by the information that he was to go as Chief Officer of *Wave Ruler* one of the RFAs ships manned by Eagle staff and due in Abadan in a day or two.

In the event Roy would be home in Liverpool with his beloved Elsie well before us. For *Wave Ruler* was also bound for the UK and would do 15 knots against our modest 11 knots.

Roy's replacement was Joe Stephens a very different type of man to Roy. Both men had done brave deeds in the past few years of war. Roy, the calm quiet family man, diffident of manner most of the time, had been awarded the OBE for his part in saving the *San Cipriano* from having her stern blown off. During a bombing attack in a Russian convoy Roy was Gunnery officer on the poop of *Cipriano*. A bomb struck the vessel on her after boatdeck, and red hot splinters fell into the open hatch of the magazine, which of course had been open to hand up cordite and shells. These splinters set fire to the cordite which began to smoulder. Roy immediately jumped down into the magazine tank and began to throw the smouldering cordite upon deck where the rest of the gun crew threw it overboard. He didn't think he had done anything remarkable, yet there is no doubt that but for his prompt action the magazine could well have blown up and taken the poop deck, gun and crew with it.

Joe Stephens, a young Scot from Dundee was brash and nervy. He had good reason. One of the stories of our Company already becoming a legend was the Malta Convoy "Operation Pedestal", in which the Tanker *Ohio* had struggled through torpedoes and bombs to deliver her cargo to a fuel starved Malta. Joe was her 3rd officer and after being on the bridge when a German bomber crashed on the foredeck right in front of him, he found himself, together with the Chief Officer, Douglas Gray, battened down in the steering flat aft, steering the ship to telephone orders from Captain Dudley

Mason on the shattered bridge. They were in the steering flat for almost 36 hours before Ohio crawled, battered and sinking into Grand Harbour.

Douglas Gray was awarded the DSO – a naval decoration and Joe got an OBE and Lloyds War Medal.

We left Abadan on a cold wintry afternoon, down the 45 miles of Shatt-al-Arab past Fao Control, into Rooka Channel, and out to the Pilot Station. Once we dropped the Iraqi Pilot Captain Smith set our course 175 degrees T and rang "Full Away on Passage". oh – so thankfully for us all!

The weather, far from being sunny and semi tropical was bad, almost like the North Sea in winter. Away to port stretched the high dark peaks of Kazakhstan, Iran's southern province, while to starboard there was only the flat land of Arabia, out of sight behind squall after squall of vicious, blinding rain. Five days later we rounded the Quoin Islands at the Entrance/Exit to the Gulf and were steaming in the warm air of the Gulf of Oman. Blue seas, blue skies, dolphins playing around the bows, there was an air of excited anticipation all over the ship. Bets were being made on when we would pick up the Pilot off Dungeness, what time we would dock, which home port would it be and best and longest odds of all on what day would we sign off the ship?

The Gulf of Aden was its usual red hot self with a shamal blowing down the Red Sea through the Straits of Bab-el- Mandeb and Perim Island like the blast from a furnace.

One of the novel pleasures of peace time sailing was meeting other ships at night. Instead of blacked out hulls in darkened convoys, it was a delight to hear the lookout men ring the focsle bell – three strokes for lights ahead, one for lights to starboard and two for lights to port. Then it was look for the red or green steaming lights to determine the other vessels course and finally call her up on Aldis lamp "what ship – where bound?" in plain language Morse code.

Ten days after clearing the Perim Island and Straits of Bab-el-Mandeb we found ourselves in a Suez Canal convoy. Halfway up the canal the tropical temperature changed right down to 45 degrees F and we all changed into our blue uniforms and threw our topees, Bombay Bowlers, into the waters of Port Said.

It was mid-December 1945 when we sailed from Port Said to encounter, not the calm Mediterranean, but weather a lot more like that of the North Sea. Travelling towards the Straits of Gibraltar we plunged head first into stormy, uncomfortable seas, to clear the Straits and return to Atlantic storms all the way till we discharged, not in the Thames, but in Holland at a little village called Hemixem, miles upstream from Antwerp. It seemed we were destined not to be home for Christmas. We paid off *San Vito* on 10th January 1946 twenty five months after sailing from the Clyde on New Year's Eve 1943.

REFLECTIONS ON A MERCHANT NAVAL WAR

When I had gone to sea in August 1940 the Battle of Britain was in its early stages. Just about that time Winston Churchill had broadcast to the nation:-

> *"We must regard the next week or so as a very important period in our history. It ranks with the days when the Spanish Armada was approaching the Channel when Drake was finishing his bowls and when Nelson stood between us and Napoleon's Grand Army at Boulogne.*
>
> *We have all read about this in our history books. But what is about to happen is on a far greater scale and of far more consequence to our life and the future of the world and its civilisation than what was happening in those Brave Old Days".*

These were stirring worlds to our people who felt that it would take time. But so long as Churchill was at our head, with good army, naval and air force officers the people of Great Britain and her Empire all standing together, Hitler would not succeed and did not.

I would like to give you some information I gleaned over the few post war years which I am sure will fill out the background to my four and a half years at sea during the Atlantic War.

From August 1940 to December 1942 I had sailed *San Conrado*, *San Cipriano*, *San Amado* and *Empire Cobbett* during the first two years where we felt we were losing, and Admiral Doenitz felt his U-boat war fare was winning. He had invented "Wolf Pack" tactics and had used the expression to one of his top commanders, Otto Kretchmer, at dinner one evening.

It was "U-boote sind die Wolfe sur See Angreifen, reissen, versinken!".

U-boats are the wolves on the sea. Attack, tear, sink.

Rudel taktil "Herd or Pack tactics".

Convoys were 35 to 45 vessels designated as SC 105 and the like "7 knots Slow Convoy". H X 221 and other letters designated Faster or Medium 9 knots.

But all convoys were invariably one or two knots slower than their designation.

From January 1942 till June 1942 360 ships were sunk totalling 2,250,000 tons at a cost of only 8 U-boats.

The Atlantic campaign swiftly began to intensify during 1940 and 1941. The *Eredona* convoy 14th and 15th March 1941 when we lost 5 ships and the Germans lost 3 U-boats, two of which were the U-boat ace captains, Otto Kretschmer in U99 and Schepke in U100 indicated how things were getting hot. Our Navy was improving its methods, Destroyers *Walker* and *Vanoc* were the killers of the two U-boats. In that same week *Wolverine* sank Gunther Prien, the third ace commander, who had penetrated Scapa Flow and sunk the *Royal Oak*.

During 1942 the average loss of ships per month was 650,000 tons, and in all of 1942 the sinking of Allied ships rose to 6,000,000 tons. Doenitz in 1942 had 212 operational boats.

In simple strategic terms the German navy could cut off the democratic arsenal of America from Great Britain and the Mediterranean and make it impossible for her to bring her vast resources to bear anywhere in the European theatre. Doenitz estimated that a monthly average of 800,000 tons of shipping would do this if it had happened. Not even the wealth and industrial might would have been any use to her, far less to Europe.

She ought to have been able to deal with Japan in the Pacific, but her entire Eastern Seaboard would have been vulnerable to the entire German Kriegsmarine of several hundred U-boats and the massive battleships.

So, to my mind, The Battle of the Atlantic came to mean so much more than the survival of Britain and her Empire.

It was The Battle of the Atlantic that was the decisive theatre of the Western half of World War II. The victor in the Atlantic would win the War.

Some statistics which are worth repeating and remembering :-

U-boats built -1,162	Merchant Seamen lost − 30,248
U-boats sunk − 786	U-boat Seamen lost − 32,000
Ships sunk − 2,828	Tonnage sunk 14,687,231 tons

As time lengthens and memories fade, it is perhaps the ordeal of the U-boat crews which stands out most starkly. They were mostly conscripts not volunteers. Of the 39,000 who served, 32,000 were lost. The highest proportion of fatalities suffered by any branch of the Armed Forces of any of the combatants.

How many of the souls must have died slowly, in suffocating terror, trapped beneath the surface of a cold ocean in the flooding hull of a crippled sub-marine. In a most cruel war theirs was the most cruel fate of all.

8
POST WAR

After my long trip, I had several months leave due to me In addition I had two months study leave, paid for by Eagle. At the time, few companies did this and I felt very lucky to be employed by such a good firm. Many of the fellows who studied with me at Leith were on the dole.

I had enough sea time in to sit for First Mate. During my long spell away from home, my romance had fizzled out. She had found someone who did not go away, promising to be gone "Only two months" and returning nineteen months later. I felt badly about it at the time, but who could really blame the girl? One of the natural hazards of going to sea.

Within a few days of starting at Leith Nautical College, I felt as if I had never been away. There was the same dusty air, smelling of the sea, ships and good tobacco. The same swearing and sweating of hard case sailor men, struggling with the complicated but ritualistic calculations of navigation and ship stability. Our instructors were men of great practical and theoretical knowledge. Both of these they poured liberally down our throats. It was intense, concentrated study. But, for those who were willing to try for a ticket, it was a worthwhile task.

Something new since I had been up for Second Mate was a course for stewards. This was run on board TS Dolphin, an old wooden wall belonging to the College and moored in Leith West Old Dock.

To give the trainees something to practise on, we students at the College were invited to have lunch on board Dolphin at one shilling per meal. In the days of rationing, this was very reasonable. The students sat in the picturesque main cabin of the old battleship, round a magnificent mahogany table. The food was plain, but well cooked and wholesome. Soup, meat, sweet, or biscuits and cheese with coffee.

The meal was served by the "makee learn" boys and we would give our order to a boy, wait patiently for about ten minutes, only to find the lad back at our sides, asking:

"What was it you wanted, sir?"

It was a good thing we had an hour and a half for lunch.

One of the compulsory subjects for all Certificates of Competency is "Signals". Surprisingly this is a subject which "fails" a lot of people. I think it is because they are inclined to regard it as too easy and do not give it enough time. The speed of sending and receiving is seven and a half words a minute in Morse code and ten words a minute in semaphore. After all the bridge watches I had kept in convoy, I found it relatively easy to get my block tests and messages in Morse correct, but Semaphore I found rather more difficult. No-one seemed to use it much at sea, yet it was part of the examination. Captain Mowat, who took us for Seamanship and Signals, was a crafty old boy. He sat in his chair in the Signals Room and gave us 95 letters and numbers in blocks of five, followed by a short paragraph from the "Scotsman". He muffled the Morse key with a duster, to prevent the additional aid of our ears in receiving the signals. The little lamp, perched like a small black banana on a high wooden platform at the end of the room, winked out its silent messages, while perspiring pupils sat in pairs, one reading, the other writing down. They had to whisper each letter and needless to say many a four letter word went with the morse.

"X ... T ... Damn! ... LV ... YBU ... Good Lor' – I'll never pass this bloody test".

Some of the fellows consistently dodged the Signals session, which always was the half-hour before lunch, preferring the bar of the "Steamboat Tavern" across the road. But I found, in the end, that knowing your signals was well worth it. How awful, to pass the major part of the written and oral exam, only to be failed on "Signals".

With a certain degree of apprehension, I again faced the ordeal of Examinations Week. On Saturday, the results. Once more I had passed and was a First Mate of a Foreign-Going ship.

As soon as I got the results I sent a telegram to Eagle to tell them I was available for sea. I had been almost six months ashore and the urge to be back at sea was strong. The long and arduous time on *SanVito* had passed into memory. If anyone had asked me about the trip, I would have said

"Oh, Not so bad. Here, did I ever tell you about that time in ... ?"

I got word in early June. "Proceed Thameshaven. Join *San Felix* as Second Officer".

Cheerfully I bade my people Goodbye and set off on the night train from Edinburgh. I had enjoyed my leave. Now I would see what the *Felix* had to offer in the way of excitement.

I reached Thameshaven the following lunchtime. It is on the Essex Marshes, near Canvey Island. The nearest village is Stamford-le-Hope, five miles away. The only way to get between the two places was either to walk, or go by taxi. I made my way out along the jetty. A stiff breeze whipped the muddy waters of the Estuary to a chop. A figure caught my eye. It was Ron Hawkins, my old Chief Officer of *San Amado*.

"Hello, sir Are you waiting to join the *Felix* too?"

"No fear". he said. I'm the berthing master here now".

We talked for a few minutes. Then he drew my attention to the ship approaching the berth.

"Look at her, Steve! God help her and all who sail in her".

True *San Felix*, as she approached the jetty was an unprepossessing sight. She was built in 1921, at that time one of the biggest tankers in the world, at 22,000 tons. But with her tall woodbine funnel, her straight up and down masts and her rusty slab sides, she was no beauty.

Immediately after the war, Eagle decided to have a new colour scheme for their ships. The funnel was, as it had always been, primrose yellow with black top and two white bands, between which strode the eagle of Mexico standing on a large black O. This design led to the fleet of Eagle ships to be known wherever they went as the "Shit-Hawk" fleet. Where the hull before had been black, it was now "purple-brown". That, I solemnly swear was the name of the colour. The masts and deck houses were a pale buff colour, known as "Eagle Oil Cream".

The man who thought up "purple-brown" must have had severe indigestion, or been colour blind. It was a most ghastly colour, which faded rapidly in the sea air. It blended most naturally with rust, so that a ship after two trips, looked a complete rust box. Within two years, I am glad to say, Eagle returned to black hulls.

My cabin on Felix was in the forward starboard corner of the bridge house. The usual fitments. Two ports, the bunk running under. Settee on forward bulkhead with the wardrobe at one end. After bulkhead with desk and wash basin. Still, she was comfortable.

I had barely got on board, when I had signed on and found myself on deck supervising cargo. As I went round the decks, I discovered that Felix was constructed differently from the more modern vessels I had been on. The modern tanker as described in Chapter One, is a three tank system of compartments. Known as the Isherwood System. Older vessels like San Felix were built on the "Summer Tank" principle.

The summer tanks were in effect saddle tanks and ran over one or two main tanks. They had their own pipeline system and also a "Drop" valve, by which the contents of the summer tank could be "Dropped" into the after main tank beneath any particular summer tank.

The valves operating the various tanks are opened and closed by wheeled stems protruding through the deck. San Felix had no wheels. The tops of the valve stems were squared off to take a ratchet spanner, which had to be carried about by the people on cargo duty. This would have been all right if the spanners fitted all the stems, but due to wear and tear, the squared stems had rounded corners so that not every ratchet fitted every valve. It was a most painful experience to rush up to a valve, drop the ratchet spanner over the head, give it a good "Jag" to start it off its seat and find the spanner slip off and crack you sharply across the shins. Right below the kneecap and always in the same spot. To get over this I quickly learned to carry a pocketful of brass "Shims" to drop into the gap between spanner head and valve stem.

Two further complications will give some idea of what it was like to work cargo on Felix. During the war she was torpedoed, but reached port without sinking. She was repaired in New York. Her damaged valves were replaced by American LEFT HAND ones – with wheels. Her forward pumproom, where she had been "bumped", was a maze of valves, some left handed, some right handed, with absolutely nothing to indicate which was which. I used to put chalk marks on the left hand ones in a despairing attempt to help myself. But the steam and condensation soon obliterated them. Normally a valve has an indicator to show whether it is closed or open, but those on San Felix were long since broken or otherwise useless.

The last complication was that at some time the Mate had the decks painted all over with red oxide. This had been coated liberally over the valve stems, so that no valve showed its distinguishing colour. When I say that on her 450 feet of tank decks there were no fewer than fifty valves protruding like so many lopped off mushrooms, the reader will begin to have some idea of what we were up against. She was a tanker officer's nightmare. I was to spend twelve months on her and discover early on that "uniform" for cargo watches was a boiler suit, into the pockets of which I could stuff a handful of shims, a torch, a small mirror, a tin of Stag jointing compound, a notebook, a pencil, and chalk and water paste. These latter were for ullage purposes. The mirror fulfilled the same purpose during the day that the torch did in the night. By reflecting the sun's rays down the sight hole I got a very good view into the tank.

It took 48 hours to discharge the ship. Then with her new crew, she sailed under the command of Captain McCarthy, through the Azores to Curacao. Her speed was nine and an onion and she took sixteen days to do the voyage. The trip was uneventful and once we reached Curacao, instead of navigating the entrance to Willemstad we berthed at Bullen Bay, the oil terminal at the Western end of the Island. No tugs were available. With the strong off-shore wind it was necessary to send two headlines ashore in the motor boat, then work the engines to bring the stern near enough to send away the stern ropes. It was a long hard heave to pull the great ship in ballast condition, alongside the jetty, in the burning heat of a tropical afternoon.

The cargo to be loaded was Naphtha, very similar to petrol. Two big flexibles were connected, the lines were set, ready for loading. One thing which is important for ship's people to know is the rate of loading. I went to the Mate.

"What's the loading rate, Tom?".

"Eighteen hundred tons an hour".

I boggled at him.

"What? In this old wreck? You'll never do it. Something is bound to give way".

But Tommy was a canny Scot.

"Och Aye, Steve. We'll do it all right. The Old Man says so".

"What about doubling up on the watches then?".

At least, I thought, more men on deck should be able to cope with any emergency.

"Na, Na, Laddie! I'll be keepin' an eye on ye".

"I hope you do, Mate, I hope you do".

By the time the first tanks were nearing the top, I realised that 1800 tons an hour was a fairly fast speed. Today loading rates of 3-4000 tons an hour are common and 1800 is relatively slow. But modern tankers have a pipeline system of large bore, with modern aids, like gauges to each tank to enable the tank flow to be controlled efficiently. On *Felix* we had only a steel measuring tape, with a brass bob at the end and six foot ullage sticks. Ullage is the expression used to denote the "Waste Space" between the surface of the oil in the tank and the deck above. The cargo tanks are calibrated so that by reading the ullage and entering a set of tables supplied by the shipbuilder, the amount of oil in the tanks may be calculated.

The ship was loading to her Summer Draft. This meant that we would be loading the "summer tanks". Once again I went in search of the Mate.

"What about the Summer Tanks, Tom? Do we load them after the main tanks are in?"

"Och, no. We'll press them up through the drop valve. The summer tank line was blanked off years ago in this ship".

I could find no words. The drop valve was a hole only six inches across. At 1800 tons, to press up the summer tanks would, I was convinced, be a disaster.

"Pressing up" is a method of loading a summer tank by keeping the level of oil in the main tank at a higher level than the eventual height desired in the summer tank. In this way the "Head" of oil in the main tank "Presses up" the level in the summer tank.

Since the final ullage for all the tanks had been worked out to be 1'3", we had to keep control of oil rushing into the ship at 1800 tons an hour and at the same time, adjust those ghastly old deck valves, so as to finish 1'3" in both main and summer tanks.

"Well! I only hope we make it" I said.

But there was worse to come. To ease the pressure we used an empty tank to "spill off" while topping up the loading tanks. This would have been fine, but the *Felix* had another trick up her rotten old sleeve. Her main pipeline, which ran round the main tanks like a "Ring main", leaked so badly and in so many places, that we began to find naphtha in all sorts of unexpected tanks. I opened a fresh set of tanks to find they already had ten feet of oil in them. *San Felix* was an old bitch.

By some miracle we loaded 18,000 tons of naphtha in ten hours. As the flexibles were being disconnected, I breathed a sigh of relief.

"Let's hope we don't come back here in a hurry".

We sailed for London River at the end of July and berthed at Thameshaven on 13th August 1946. When the ship was "Opened up" for discharge, Naphtha was found in all the compartments normally kept free from cargo. The cofferdams were half full of it. The pumprooms were over the pump tops in it. The internal structure of that old ship was a complete honeycomb.

This time leaving London, we embarked twelve passengers. In 1946 passages to the West Indies by air and sea were very hard to get. There were lots of people whose interests in the Caribbean had been neglected during the war and who now were anxious to get out there. There were also the families of Oil Company employees who wanted to get out to their husbands and fathers. Naturally only those with influence could get a passage such as we provided. Those with shares in Shell, perhaps?. We certainly had a mixed bag.

The passenger deck was the boat deck, midships. It had five double cabins and "the boudoir", as the owners suite was irreverently called. There was little or no deck space. Captain McCarthy, whose lounge was on the passenger deck, kindly gave it up for the use of passengers.

During the several voyages I made on *Felix*, she carried passengers each time. We had a crusty old colonel, his wife and daughter, whose opinion of the National Coal Board, which had taken over his mine in the North East was blistering. A wartime "boffin" whose tales of poisoned cigarettes and wrist watch A/P bombs were fascinating if gruesome. His wife, a handsome lady of fifty, went nowhere on the ship, without clutching a large handbag, in which we swore were the family jewels. We carried women and children, wives of employees in the oilfields of Venezuela and Trinidad. We carried hard bitten Oilmen, who had drilled for oil in the mountains of Persia and the rich black lands of Texas and Oklahoma. These fellows drank pints of whisky and played poker, morning, noon and night.

Four months of my twelve month stint on San Felix had passed, before she began finally to fold up. So far as her deck officers were concerned, she was a good enough old ship. Our only nightmares were the loading and discharging of her. And it is amazing what you can get used to. With the engineers it was a different story. She was an oil burning steam turbine ship, having five scotch boilers, supplying steam to a turbine, which drove through reduction gearing, the four blade single screw. The boilers started to give trouble. Leaky tubes. In a Scotch boiler the water is heated by the hot gases from the furnace passing through a series of smoke tubes, which are surrounded by the water. If a smoke tube corrodes or fractures water is enabled to get back into the furnace. The leaky tube is "stopped" by a special tube stopper, which is inserted in the tube and seals it off. Now the engineers were finding that this had to be done more and more frequently.

A modern steam turbine ship is very handy to manoeuvre, as her engines can be moved from ahead to astern quite quickly. But in the early Turbine vessels this was very much slower. In San Felix's case, it took three full minutes to move from an ahead to an astern movement. A lot can happen in three minutes, as the following anecdote illustrates.

San Felix was in Emmastad, to load a part cargo of petrol. An oil port such as this has very naturally stringent rules about leaking of oil on to the harbour. It was not long before the authorities were on the quay, to complain about Felix polluting the harbour and to threaten the Master with a whopping fine. Loading was stopped at once and arrangements made for the ship to proceed to Bullen Bay. Within half an hour the pilot was on board and we were at stations. There were no tugs in Curacao at that time and all shipping movements had to be done using the ship's engines and the prevailing wind. To get away from Bernardwerfe and to sea, San Felix had to make a complete S-turn.

Normally this would have been fairly easy. A certain amount of backing and filling would be necessary to get round the bows of the ship moored at Oost pier, but in the main it was easy enough.

But not for the old lady. The Captain warned the Pilot, a young Dutchman, that the engines were slow. But to no avail. He completely misjudged both the strength of the breeze and San Felix's manoeuvring powers. Instead of travelling smoothly round the turn and into the channel, San Felix sagged inexorably, broadside on to the anchor chains of the Norwegian tanker at Oost Pier.

The Mate of the Norwegian, thinking to lessen the shock of the two ships colliding, slacked away both cables which held his ship stern on to her berth. This had the effect of making the Norwegian ship fall off before the wind and San Felix's relentless pressure, so that she ended up lying athwart the bows of a third tanker Clydefield lying at Oceaanpier.

Somehow Felix extricated herself and steamed ponderously out of Emmastad, leaving in her wake the shambles of her passing. No sooner had she docked at Bullen Bay, than two notes of protest came on board. One from the Norwegian and one from the Clydefield. In addition, a letter from the Harbour Authority in Emmastad, charging Felix with pollution of the port.

The Captain shut himself in his room to ponder the issue. Meanwhile the leaky rivets which were the cause of the trouble had to be caulked, before loading. The tank affected had to be made gas-free, no small job when the rest of the ship contained cargo. It was done and the remaining cargo loaded in the inimitable fashion of San Felix. When the outline of Curacao dropped below the horizon, everyone on board breathed more easily. It had been a hectic stay in port. We ought to have saved our breath. Scarcely had we cleared Mona Passage than the refrigerator went on the blink. This was no ordinary small domestic fridge but two big rooms containing 1,000 pounds of meat, fish and offal. Apart from a few days supply all of this had to be dumped.

In the ensuing days, the speed of San Felix, never very good, began to drop. The old trouble in her boilers had flared up again. this time, much more seriously. So many tubes were beginning to leak, in each boiler, that the affected boiler had to be blown down and tube stoppers inserted in the leaking tubes, to seal them off. There is of course a limit to the number of tubes that can be put out of use in any one boiler before it becomes inoperative. In the ordinary way one leaky boiler would have been little trouble. It could have been shut off and the remaining four would have been adequate for steaming the ship. But now each boiler produced its crop of leaky tubes. No sooner was one boiler shut down, the tubes stopped and flashed up again, than another would give trouble. Day by day our speed dropped, from nine to seven. From seven to five knots. To further aggravate our condition the weather deteriorated into a South-east gale, force nine. This was a bit unusual, as most of the bad weather on our route was from South West and North West gales. At least a Westerly gale would have been blowing us home. The old tanker, like some grotesque half tide rock, rolled endlessly in the trough of the great seas. Her bows pointed defiantly to the North East, but scarcely a mile she travelled in that direction. She had not enough speed to keep her bows up into the wind. Gauging her speed by ship's log was useless. The log line hung nearly up and down in the water. I had to resort to other means. I measured a 400ft length of her deck, by dropping a piece of wood over from the forward mark and walking aft to the second mark, I timed the passage of the piece of wood between the two. From this I could calculate the ship's speed, as the big propeller turned all too slowly under her ugly old counter. One and a quarter knots was all she was making.

San Felix was a member of the Voluntary Fleet of Weather Observer Ships whose officers report every six hours to "Weather, Telex Dunstable". Their reports are used to help in the preparation of weather forecasts by the Met Office. Since it was taking us a week to pass from one side of the Azores to the other, the Captain decided to stop sending the reports.

"Dunstable will be thinking we're a shore station," he said gruffly. "Forget about sending them in for now".

He was nothing if not resourceful. At breakfast one day, after we had rolled till it seemed we would turn over, he announced,

"Mr Mate we're going to rig a sail on the poop"

"A sail, sir?" spluttered Tommy, choking on his toast. "We have no sails"

"Ah," leered the Master. "But we have plenty of old canvas down in the hold, have we not?".

"Yes, sir".

"Well, get it up after breakfast and send it along aft. We can use the pipeline derrick for a topping lift. It'll bring her head to wind and ease this bloody rolling".

Since all hands were tired of the incessant movement, they set to work with a will under the Captain's orders. By eight bells there was a tiny green triangle of canvas filling out bravely but ineffectually in the gale. It had not the slightest effect on bringing the ship's head to wind. If anything, the increased wind surface made her roll worse, if I had thought that possible.

The eternal rolling was exhausting after many days. My legs ached from the constant effort to brace my body to meet the ship. No one was seasick any more. They had long ago got over that. They were sick of the sea, if you like. In bed the only way to get to sleep, was to lie with one knee drawn up and pressing against the bunk board, while your back lay against the bulkhead. Even so an extra big roll commonly threw you clean out of bed to land on the floor, a cursing bruised bundle of sleep and blankets.

From the bridge the sea was an awe-inspiring sight. Its entire surface was broken into curling whitecaps, torn in the instant of their formation into spindrift, lying along the backs of the huge waves in thick foaming streaks.

From one wave to its neighbour could be anything up to two hundred feet. Very often it was more. The height of the waves from trough to crest was anything from fifteen to thirty feet. The horizon lurched sickeningly from the extremity of one roll, through sixty degrees to the extremity of the other. On the wing of the bridge it was like being on one end of a seventy foot seesaw, as the wing swooped from one roll to the other. To increase the sensation further, the liquid cargo followed, inside the hull, some moments behind the ship herself. Thus, instead of a steady roll, like that of a cargo vessel, *Felix* would roll, then, when you thought the limit was reached, the oil caught up and she would give a little lurch and hold the angle for several seconds before returning, with a wild rushing swoop, through the horizontal, to repeat the performance on the other side.

"She'll roll the sticks out of her yet"

remarked the Bosun morosely, as he eyed the 125 foot masts gyrating madly over his head.

Being so low in the water, the main decks, on which we officers spent to much time in port, were continually submerged in salt water, rushing hissing, forming round deck obstructions, tank coamings and pipelines, finally gurgling out through the scuppers and freeing ports.

All things come to an end. The weather blew itself out, the boilers were kept going by the heroic efforts of our engineers and the ship crept imperceptibly on her way home. 92 miles a day. 96 miles a day. Finally 120 miles a day.

The London Office had been advised of our predicament and we received orders to proceed to Falmouth. On the morning of Guy Fawkes, 1946, *San Felix* crept round the Manacles and the tugs made fast to her blunt rusty bows.

An oil-blackened figure, its eyes red-rimmed with exhaustion came on the bridge. No one would have recognised the usually trim Chief Engineer.

"Tugs fast yet, Cap'n?"

"Yes, Chief. Just made fast now".

"Good. The last boiler packed in five minutes ago. You've got no engines"

The tugs and pilot manoeuvred a sea weary *Felix* and her crew into Crossroads Anchorage, in the River Fal. Normally the trip from the West Indies took sixteen days. It had taken *San Felix* thirty five.

Next day she went alongside for repairs to her old and sorely tried boilers. Enough to get her up the Channel to London, discharge and return to Falmouth. She was there three days before setting off for London. It took a further three to make Thameshaven.

The reason for the parlous state of *San Felix* was that the Company were in two minds about scrapping her. On the one hand she was 24 years old, a venerable age for a tanker. On the other, after losses suffered during the war, tanker tonnage was in great demand, but to give the old lady a really good "Beat up" would cost a lot of money. So we officers had to keep her staggering on, being patched up as required.

After discharging at Thameshaven, we went out to the Estuary for a week's tank cleaning. On the way she narrowly missed ramming the bank, due to her general unhandiness in narrow waters. The starboard anchor had to be dropped to brake her headlong rush for the shore. When it was hove up another length of anchor chain, from some ship, was found wrapped round her cable. It took a few hours messing about on a cold Focsle with wires and bits of chain to free this. By the time we finally anchored in Black Deep, it had long since grown dark. So far out were we, that no land was visible.

The usual time taken in 1946 to clean tanks was 36-48 hours. "Cooking" the compartments with high pressure steam, in sections of three or four at a time, was followed by washing out and ventilating with wind chutes. With the poor steam pressure available it took us several days, swinging round our anchor in the cold waters of the Estuary.

So bad was this pressure that only two compartments could be steamed at one time. All told the ship had 32 tanks, apart from pumprooms and cofferdams, to be made gas-free. An officer could check the effectiveness of the steaming out process, by the tempera-ture of the deck beneath his feet. If it was too hot to hold his hand on the bare steel, the job was going well. If it was cool, the process was useless, for it meant that the steam, instead of "killing" the gas, was condensing and lying in the tank bottom as water. Any tank under steam had the pump kept on it, at draining speed, to suck out condensate and prevent the tank from cooling.

The second night of the gas-freeing, I came on watch at 2.0. am. I went round the decks, testing with my hand. They were stone cold. I looked at the deck lights. So low was the dynamo that the filaments glowed like little red wires. The steam must be virtually non-existent. I went aft to the engine room to see what was happening. As I entered the engine room casing I heard the crash of falling wood and the stentorian voice of a fireman, yelling:

"Look out below! Timber-r-r-!"

The engine room was lit by a few electric torches and some slush lamps. I made my way down the long steel ladder leading to the control platform, some thirty feet below. As I neared the bottom a man's figure appeared in the beam of my torch. It was a fireman, but he seemed curiously foreshortened. Had he been injured? He seemed to have no knees.

"Who is it?" he asked, shading his eyes from the glare of my torch.

"The second Mate. What's going on?" I stepped down beside him.

"Mind the water, sir".

Then I found what had made the man appear so short. He was up to his knees in black oily water.

"Good grief" I exclaimed. "Where's the Chief?"

He jerked an oily thumb in the direction of the stokehold. I splashed my way through the water, between the black bellies of two boilers and into the stokehold. It was a scene straight from Dante's Inferno. Oil blackened, sweating engineers were slaving to get the fuel pump working. So low had the steam fallen that the Chief had to resort to burning old dunnage wood in the furnaces, (hence the cry of timber) in order to raise steam sufficiently to operate the fuel pump, which pumped fuel to the burners of the furnaces. It sounds incredible, but it is true. Here and there on the stokehold plates oil soaked waste, discarded after being used as a flashing up torch, burned with a cold blue flame, illuminating the desperate features of the engine room staff. I did not speak to the Chief. He would come and tell me when he had steam enough.

Fourteen days after her first arrival in Falmouth *San Felix* returned there for drydock and overhaul. Her crew were paid off in November 1946, after she had been manoeuvred into the graving dock off Silley Weir and Cox. So poor was her stream pressure that her headropes were hooked on to the buffers of two dock locomotives, who pulled her gently but firmly into her berth. As she took the blocks I could almost hear her sigh, like an old lady who has come to the end of a long and tiring journey, and who now looks for a rest – a bit of peace and quiet.

I was Duty Officer that first night. It was a fine mild evening. About Midnight I went on the bridge to check something. Captain McCarthy called to me.

"Second Mate, come and watch this".

He indicated the flying bridge stretching away into the darkness. We waited. Into view came Whisky the ship's cat. Her usual quarters were the Captain's cabin, but during the past weeks of the voyage she had deserted him for a fireman's room. In this she had six kittens. The old man had given her up for lost, surrendering to the whim of a lady. Now here she was, bringing each of her kittens, one at a time in her mouth, back to his room.

I stood by the ship for almost three months in Falmouth, over Christmas 1946, and New Year. I had no desire to go home, and was content to get to know the little Cornish town, whose steep streets and lovely countryside were so restful after the fury of the sea. Indeed I got a kick out of going down to the beach during a gale and watching the breakers piling so relentlessly on the sand. To sleep sound in a bunk which remained steady was a reassuring experience.

During her stay in Falmouth *San Felix* was used as a kind of transit camp by the Company. At that time, personnel were difficult to come by, and anyone applying for a position with Eagle was immediately secured by being sent to join the *Felix*, till a ship in commission was available. This meant that the population of *Felix* was constantly changing sometimes being as high as her full complement, and at others a mere handful of twenty six or so. As Officer in Charge of her, it was my job to keep the ship's accounts, to draw the money for the wages each week and pay everybody, to complete all the paperwork, from income tax to allotments, and present the head office each Saturday with a portage bill, correctly balanced to the last penny. I knew sweet Fanny Adams about ship's accounts when I started, but could reel the lot off after several weeks.

9

RIO DE JANEIRO

On 20th January 1947 we signed on for the forthcoming voyage. Re-tubed, the ship's boilers were brand new. On deck, nothing much had been done. A few of the worst leaks in the tank bulkheads had been repaired. But it was like it says in the Bible – You can't patch an old coat with new cloth. And San Felix was a ragged old overcoat of a ship.

We went back to Bullen Bay. After our long absence the locals thought the ship had been scrapped, and were delighted to see her again. As one of the Dutch Cargo wallahs said,

"Widout Zasn Velix Bullenbaai is noddings!"

From Curacao we went down to South America. It took us three weeks to make the trip to Rio de Janeiro. This famous port is one of the most beautiful natural harbours in the world. It looks as if the huge landlocked bay has, in the distant past, been the crater of an extinct volcano. The rocks and nearby hills are basaltic in composition. The approach to the harbour is made through a channel between two islands and once the ship is through the gap, a wonderful vista opens out before your eyes. On the port hand the sweep of Copacabana Beach with its magnificent hotels and homes is, quite literally, the "String of Pearls". By the time the vessel has reached her anchorage in Quarantine, Sugar Loaf Mountain has been passed and the whole of the inner bay lies in breathtaking loveliness. Ships of all nations crowd the waters of the harbour. Beyond, like some fantastic theatrical background, rise the serrated black peaks of the distant mountains.

The ceremony of the "Official Visit" was now enacted. In most ports of the world, the various authorities who have dealings with ships come on board in the following order. First is the health officer, to prove that the ship is healthy. Then comes the customs,

San Felix in Bullen Bay.

the fire and safety officer, the ship's agent and the cargo representatives. Once the ship has been declared healthy, these people can come on board at any time and in any order. Up a pilot ladder or over the side in whatever fashion they choose. But not in Latin America. Here the Accommodation Ladder must be rigged, as in passenger ships. The port authority launch comes ponderously alongside, and the first man up the gangway is the port health officer. He is followed by at least two of his minions, carrying his briefcase, and perhaps his umbrella. He is greeted by the chief officer, if not the master. Though this is done with ill grace, it must be done, for these petty officials have it in their power to delay and fine the ship, more or less at their whim. A sad state of affairs. Each of these officials has to be "squared". That is, given a gift of some kind. Usually duty free cigarettes or spirits. Even the customs officers expect this. Only after this visit has been made can the ship proceed to her berth. Sometimes a ship will wait as long as five hours for the official visit to be made. But she can not do a thing about it. I call it holding a ship or company to ransom.

The Shell Terminal was set on a small island in the middle of the harbour, about six miles from Rio. I did not bother to go to town. It seemed not worth the effort, for the only means of getting to the mainland was rather unreliable old ferry.

San Felix lived up to her reputation for getting into trouble.

The jetty she was alongside was a rickety pile structure. When it came time for her to leave, and her blunt bows swung away from their moorings, the propeller refused to turn. When the tugs towed her clear of the berth, a long piece of broken pile from the jetty floated up from between the propeller arch. It had caught there when she was swinging off the jetty.

It was on the return voyage that I experienced the effect of a total eclipse of the sun. The ship was off the South American Coast, during November 1947.

I left *San Felix* in Thameshaven on 23rd June 1947, twelve months all but five days from joining her. It had been an exciting year, of storms, breakdowns, passengers, and sheer hard work. She had been an intractable old cow, a floating wreck. But she had been a happy ship. This is quite a common paradox. Ask a sailor what his happiest ship was and he will almost always mention some broken down old tramp. I had learned an invaluable lesson for a seaman. To improvise, to make use of my brains and common sense, to make the best use of whatever is available, whether it be men, materials or the elements.

"There's no such word at sea – ".

I spent the next two months enjoying the summer at home. I still had not enough sea time to go for Master, and at the end of my leave, looked forward once more to my next ship. She turned out to be *San Wilfrido* ex *Empire Cobbett* the old Ministry Tanker I had sailed in during 1943. Renamed, and acquired by Eagle, she was to have me as her Second Officer for the ensuing months.

I joined her in North Shields, in Smith's Docks. When I saw her, she was just as ugly to look at, in spite of her Eagle livery. At sea, I knew she would be just as dirty a ship, so far as shipping water was concerned. But she carried 15,000 tons of cargo and in 1947 this was the main thing.

Her Master was Captain Edward Shotton. He had been captured by the *Scharnhorst* when in command of *San Casimiro* and had spent four years in a POW camp.

As I signed on and took my gear aboard, up a grimy gang plank, I reflected that life was going to be the same old routine. Watches, navigation, rolling across the ocean. A wave of revulsion swept over me. What was I, a young reasonably intelligent man, doing aboard a ship like this? I could be working ashore, in some office or factory. Going home at night to a comfortable bed, which stayed steady and having weekends to do as I pleased. Just look around you Mate. A rusty expanse of tank deck, covered with welding cables, bits of metal, timber and the amazing, heterogeneous collection of shipyard junk, which every ship in a repair yard seems to accumulate. My cabin, when I got to it, was a mess. The previous Second Mate was busy packing for home. I went along to the office. The Chief Officer was Frank Wyborne, who had been my Chief Officer on the same ship four years previously. One of the rarer coincidences of life at sea. Two men sailing on the same ship, within a short space of time. I felt immensely cheered by our meeting. The black wave of depression was suddenly lifted.

Another thing which cheered me – and the other officers – was a buzz that we were to carry two lady passengers to Curacao.

"Where on earth do we accommodate them?" was the question.

We had two spare cabins at the back of the bridge, formerly used by the extra Radio Officers in the war.

"Anyway, knowing the type of passengers we carried on the *Felix*, they'll most likely be a couple of wealthy duchesses" I said to the Third Mate.

On the morning of sailing day, the Third Mate burst into my cabin.

"Come and see the Old Duchesses – they're just coming aboard now".

I followed him on deck.

Coming up the gangway were two dainty, attractive young women. Their air of delicate femininity contrasted vividly with the masculine atmosphere of the repair yard. Appreciative whistles followed their progress. Behind them came the Old Man, a surprised but gratified expression on his rubicund face.

Mid Atlantic on *San Wilfrido.*

Nina was a tall, willowy blonde from London. She had a peaches and cream complexion, and a languid, sophisticated manner which, however was only a cover up for a very nice, rather timid girl.

Christine was a petite, well shaped Scots girl. Also blonde and with an alert, wary look about her, as if she expected always to have her leg pulled. Both were on their way to join their husbands, Christine to Punta Cardon, Nina to San Lorenzo in the Venezuelan Oil Fields.

Now came the moment of crisis. Nina had a dachshund and a right Percy he looked. No dogs or animals were normally carried on Eagle ships. But, after Nina had declared in the Shipping Office, quite firmly, that if Percy didn't go, neither did she, Captain Shotton relented, and Percy was "signed on", along with the girls, at one shilling a day.

With a crowd of young officers, and two such personable young women it was inevitable that the trip would be diverting. Captain Shotton kept a fatherly and discreet eye out for any "Monkey business" but there was none. We respected the ladies too much. But we kidded and pulled their legs unmercifully. All the yarns about what happens at sea, were hauled out, dusted off, and presented to the girls, by poker faced officers, as gospel truth. We soon found out that Nina, for all her veneer of worldliness and sophistication, would swallow any yarn however preposterous, but Christine would take most of them with a large pinch of salt.

Our first Sunday at sea, we were at breakfast in the saloon. As I rose from the table, I said to no one in particular,

"Don't forget, church service at eleven o'clock".

"Oh yes" said the Third Mate, "Must press my uniform".

The girls dressed in sweaters and slacks, looked up.

"You don't have a church service on a tanker, surely?" said Christine.

"On this one we do" I said firmly, "Captain Shotton is a great Bible puncher".

"What shall we wear?" asked Nina, a trifle anxiously.

"Your best clothes" I suggested, excusing myself.

"Remember – eleven o'clock in the saloon".

I thought no more of the matter, I felt sure that someone would tell them it was only a joke.

To my consternation, at half past ten, Sparks called me out on deck.

"Get an eyeful of this" he said.

Strolling gracefully up and down the long main deck were Christine, Nina and Percy. The ladies were dolled up to the nines and looked really delicious. Nina even carried a prayer book.

"Crikey!" I gulped "What do I do now?"

Fortunately for me, the weather, which had been threatening fog, closed right in.

At lunch Christine eyed me narrowly.

"What happened to the church service?"

"Oh" I said airily "The Captain has to be on the bridge all the time in fog. Otherwise we'd have had it".

But I could see she didn't believe me.

It took Percy a long time to get his sea legs. As the ship rolled, he would run with the roll. No matter what obstruction came in his way, he seemed to have no way of stopping himself. His little short legs would go ten to the dozen, as he charged across the ship, yelping pitiably in terror. Then as the ship rolled the other way, the reverse would happen.

One day, at lunch, the conversation turned to ghosts. We discovered that Nina, who did not believe in them, nevertheless was firmly convinced of the power of mediums. She remarked that she had visited one or two seances.

Captain Shotton spoke up.

"You are a bit of a Medium, aren't you Chief?"

Jack Scholes, the stocky, dark Chief Engineer looked round the table. He had a way of looking at people which could be curiously unnerving. Slowly, he spoke.

"Aye, I am. But I have to have a rapport with someone".

Again his black eyes bored into Ninas. She blushed, then said defiantly.

"All right, Captain, I'll try with him".

"Thank you Mrs. Pocock" said the Captain gravely "Once we get through the Azores we'll hold a seance".

San Wilfrido
(the old *Empire Cobbett*)
sporting the "goalpost"
masts which held the anti
torpedo nets in place.

The Chief's cabin was rigged up for the occasion. A loudspeaker was wired beneath the settee and a mike led from it to the bathroom. A blue bulb was fitted in the ceiling light and a "Ghost", made of a coat hanger and a white sheet, was arranged to be whipped in and out of a porthole by a pulley and lanyard.

In the second dog watch the seance was begun. What a transformation had been wrought in the Chief. By skilful use of an old cloak from the engine room rag bag, an oakum wig and cotton wool pads stuffed inside his cheeks, he was a fearful sight. With talc rubbed on his face and a torch burning upwards from his chest, he looked ghastly. The storekeeper, whose voice the ladies were unlikely to recognise had been enrolled to stand behind the bathroom door, mike in hand, and answer the questions of the chief, who sat at the table immediately in front of the door.

We all sat solemnly round the table and spread our hands, fingers touching, palms downward. Nina was next to me. I could feel her trembling in her thin dress, but whether from excitement or apprehension, I could not tell.

Outside the porthole waited the two cadets with the "piece de resistance".

The cabin lights dimmed. There was silence for a moment. The medium spoke.

"Oh, spirit of Lake Maraicabo" he quavered, "can you hear me?"

There came an unearthly whistling from somewhere in the room. A falsetto voice, disembodied, eery, shrilled out.

"Ye-e-es-s- I can hear you" Between Nina and I, Percy growled.

"We are here to ask your help. Can you give it us?"

"I sh-a-l-l try".

Questions and answers went round the table. We had previously arranged this in order to give some authenticity to the proceedings. Soon it was the turn of Christine.

"What kind of place is Cardon?" she asked.

"Very nice. Very lovely".

"Will I like it?"

"Your husband awaits. I say no more".

A few more questions by officers, then it was Nina's turn. Still trembling she asked, as had Christine,

"What kind of place is San Lorenzo?"

"Ghastly" said the spirit "Snakes and other creatures abound."

"Will I like it?" persisted Nina.

"For a time you will detest it. But, – Ah – wait. I can see great happiness for you".

"What kind of happiness?"

But the spirit was fading.

"Great happiness … " The voice trailed off.

The medium spoke.

"Can you manifest yourself, O Spirit?"

"I – can – try – " Faintly.

"We await your coming".

There came a scream from Nina. Percy dashed from below her chair, hackles raised and snarling defiantly.

In the centre of the room, there danced a white form. Eerily it jigged up and down, before disappearing out of the open port. Christine was lightning quick. She was out of the cabin and on deck after the "ghost". But the boys were ready. They had whipped both line and sheet and fled below to the 'Tween' deck.

Christine came back in, crestfallen at her failure to find any evidence that the spook had been staged. We were impressed by her courage in going to investigate.

Some days later the girls gave us a return show, aided by the Chief and the Steward. An awful lot of toilet rolls were all at once required by the ladies. No matter how we tried to find out they kept their secret.

This time the smoke room was the scene of operations. First the Chief and the Steward gave a silhouette show, followed by a sand dance. The Chief was a stocky, plump man, the Steward thin and raw-boned. It was a perfect Laurel and Hardy act.

The gramophone began to churn out a tango. The lights changed and into the smoke room danced two Hawaiian Lovelies.

Now the secret of the toilet rolls was revealed. The rustling grass skirts of the girls were made out of paper, fathoms of it, patterned in red blue and green polka dots.

Amid cheers and wolf whistles, Nina and Christine gyrated slowly and beautifully, it was a rousing success.

After a glass of beer, and the girls had changed, we danced on deck in the moonlight, as the ship rolled easily in the Trades. The gramophone was old and scratchy. The tunes dated, but with a lovely dancing partner, under the stars, who cared?

When the girls left the ship in Bullen Bay, we were sorry to see them go. For a little while they had lightened our days. The trip out had taken no time at all. We hoped they had enjoyed our company.

*   *   *

Captain Shotton left us at the end of that trip. Our new Master was Captain Pritchard. A stocky, twinkling eyed Welshman, he was a different type to Captain Shotton. Where Shotton had been pleasant, though reserved in manner, Pritchard was ebullient and impulsive.

We dropped the pilot off Dover during my watch. Captain Pritchard rang "Full Away" then came over to me.

"Keep her down the middle of the Channel, Second Mate. Call me when we're a hundred miles off the Azores".

This was unusual. The normal procedure was for the Navigating Officer to lay off the courses on the Great Circle chart, show them to the Master who checked them. Then lay off the Mercator rhumb courses and again have the Master check them. But it lent a new sense of responsibility to me as Navigator. I felt that the navigation of the ship really was in my hands.

We went to Trinidad. to Point Fortin, the United British Oilfields terminal, some thirty eight miles south of Port of Spain. The jetty was about half a mile long and carried the pipelines only. To get ashore we had to use a launch.

I went ashore in the morning to do some shopping. Here was the real Tropics. The township was tiny, a cluster of native shops and stores down each side of a street. Donkeys and people slept and dozed in the shade. I bought a few things at the Company Commissary, and strolled back to the oil depot. Tall mahogany trees flanked the road. At intervals, fine modern bungalows stood back off the road, each in its large garden, filled with flaming bougainvillaea, scarlet hibiscus and other exotic flowers. People must have a good life here.

I was about to go on watch at 2p.m. when the Captain who had also been ashore, sent for me.

"Get changed, Second Mate, we're going ashore. Important".

"But I've my watch to do" I protested.

"The Third Mate will do it. I want you to come with me".

I went in search of the Third Mate. He was not amused, but an order from the Master was not to be disregarded.

"I'm sorry, old man, but it's Captain's orders" I said. "Don't know when I'll be back".

"He's an interfering old buzzard" said the Third Mate, feelingly.

Once ashore, Pritch hailed a taxi.

"Take us to the Pitch Lake Manager's house" he said to the beaming West Indian driver.

"Yas, Boss! Shuah ting, Mister Captain".

And off we went through the mahogany plantations, the slim trunks towering upwards to a leaf green ceiling. Pritch grinned at me.

"Still wondering where we're going?" he asked.

"Yes sir".

"I'm taking you to meet some Scotch people" he said. "When I told them I had a porridge eating Second Mate, they wanted to meet you".

So much for the important job he had wanted me for I thought wryly. The Third Mate would be pleased when he found out.

The taxi stopped outside a large and beautiful house. Bungalow was too poor a description for it. It was a small mansion, standing on eight foot stilts. A wide staircase of polished mahogany gave access to its broad, screened veranda.

We were greeted by Mr. Ross and his gracious wife. Both in their mid-fifties, they came from Edinburgh. Ross was a tall handsome man of immense charm. His wife was equally kind and both did their best to make us at home.

Later, Mr. Ross took me to see the Pitch Lake. It is a natural phenomenon, an actual lake of pitch. I was told it was one end of a "Pipe" of pitch, which ran under the sea and whose other end rose to the surface in the Colombian Jungle.

It looked for all the world like a marsh, rather disappointing in appearance. On its surface, here and there grew tussocks of grass and small bushes. A good part of it was covered with water which had to be pumped off from time to time.

The operation of extracting the pitch was simplicity itself. A light railway ran out from the shore on to the surface of the lake, to the working area. Here a gang of cheerful West Indians dug out great lumps of raw pitch from the lake and dumped them in little trucks. These were then pushed back to shore and their contents placed in large boilers, called stills, so that decaying vegetation such as wood and other extraneous matter would float to the top where it could be removed. The pitch was run off in sequence from each still, through steam heated troughs, and poured, a dollop at a time into mud lined barrels made of wood. These were then placed in slings on an aerial ropeway, which took them over the ridge and down to the ship loading at the jetty.

"Fancy this as a job, my boy?" asked Mr. Ross, on the way back.

"I'm afraid I'm no engineer, sir. I know nothing about machinery".

The Manager looked at me searchingly.

"Hmm. Pity. I've rather taken a liking to you".

Thus one of the best opportunities of my life slipped from my grasp.

When we got back to the house, Captain Pritchard had gone off to the club. This was rather naughty of him, as Mrs. Ross had arranged a dinner for us. Her daughter had joined us for the meal. To sit on a veranda, under the moon, sipping Drambuie, and enjoying the conversation of kindly, intelligent people, was I thought, a wonderful experience.

At last it was time for me to take my leave. I rose and thanked my host and hostess for their kindness. Outside, the taxi from the Agency was waiting to transport me from this dream world back to the reality of life on a ship.

I neared the tanker in the darkness, after a trek along part of the pier and climbing into the waiting launch. It seemed as if she was magically transformed into a passenger ship. It couldn't be what I had had to drink at the Ross's. I rubbed my eyes and looked again. There were men and women all over the ship.

I met the Mate on the quayside. He shrugged his shoulders resignedly and indicated the ship over his shoulder with a jerk of his thumb.

"Pritch is throwing a party" he said "All over the ship"

"I can see that" I grinned.

"You won't grin like that when you see your cabin" said the Mate. "It's full of people listening to the big fight".

I climbed the ladder to the accommodation, pushing past crowds of men and women. All through the alleyways and cabins they were listening to a fight from America on the ships broadcast. My own cabin contained seven or eight people listening to my radio and drinking my beer.

"Come in" I said sarcastically "Make yourselves at home".

"Actually old boy" said one chap, somewhat abashed, "We have done. The Captain said we'd find a case of beer in your wardrobe. We kept a couple for you".

"That's handsome of you" I said, but I was cooling off.

It wasn't the fault of the people. It was that old devil, Pritch. I went upstairs to the chartroom to have a smoke. As I stepped into the darkened wheelhouse, I heard a soft gasp of alarm and a slight scuffle. In the same instant I smelt a girl's perfume.

"Crikey" I thought, gloomily, "They're all over the bloody place".

At three o'clock in the morning a tugboat came out from shore and collected the residents of Point Fortin. It had been a whale of a party.

At one stage in the proceedings I tried to see the Captain. His room was packed tight with people. In the middle stood Pritch, glass in hand, his eyes twinkling as he talked with the prettiest woman in the room. He wasn't a bad guy. He just loved people.

*   *   *

On my next and last trip on San Wilfrido we went back to Rio de Janeiro and Santos. We arrived right at the height of "Carnavale", that festival which precedes Lent. The whole city of Rio was en fete, and in spite of our long hours of cargo duty I felt I must see this. A few sweet words in the ear of the Mate, and Sparks, the Third Mate and myself found ourselves ashore at ten o'clock that evening. This was the best time of the day, for the festivities were at their height. We walked up the Avenida de Rio Branco, surely one of the most beautiful thoroughfares in the world, and that evening even more so. It is a wide duel carriageway, lined with trees and fabulous shops and stores. All were lighted for the occasion and a myriad of fairy lights glistened between the tree branches and lamp standards. The noise was indescribable. Imagine hundreds of happy people, in their best clothes or in fancy dress, doing the Samba all together as they promenaded up and down the street. It was impossible actually to walk, you had to samba. A long procession of floats, lorries and sleek American coupes, moved slowly up one side and down the other, bearing wonderful set pieces and beautiful girls. One I remember was of Venus, a gorgeous Latin beauty, whose attendants were little girls each sitting in a lotus flower illuminated from within. At the top of the Avenida, where it reaches the sea front, stands the Opera House. Up its broad steps moved a galaxy of dinner suited men and beautifully gowned women. After a rest on the sea front, we set off to come down the other side.

Halfway down there was an arcade in which stood a queue of people in fancy dress, waiting to have their photographs taken. We went in, to have a spell from the continual samba. Sparks dug me in the ribs.

"Get a load of those two, Steve".

I did. Two lovely Portuguese girls, dressed in crinolines of palest blue. In their hair, high Spanish combs, over which hung black lace mantillas. Even as we gazed at them, they smiled tentatively over their fans. We decided to speak to them. It was very difficult. The only Spanish I know is "Se Prohibe Fumare" – it is forbidden to smoke! Even Sparks, who could speak Spanish, was at a loss, for they spoke Portuguese, the Linga Franca of Rio. However we managed to get along well enough with signs and smiles. The only fly in the ointment was the Third Mate, the young bearded Londoner. I tried to persuade him to go back to the ship and do my watch for me. But he was adamant. So, the best we could do was to make a date with the girls for the following night.

"Same time, same place".

The girls looked puzzled. Why should their escorts suddenly want to go off and leave them. But there it was.

Next evening Sparks and I shot ashore at the double. We had to meet them at half past Midnight in the arcade. Impatiently we shoved our way up the street towards the arcade. Sweating from our efforts, we reached the spot. A seething mass of humanity filled the arcade. We hung around for half an hour but it was hopeless. Even if the ladies had turned up, we could never have found them.

The following evening, the last of Carnavale, we sailed out of Rio. From the peak of Sugar Loaf a gigantic firework display showered its streams of red, blue and green light. Higher, on its mountain top, the floodlit cross of Christ stood in the darkening sky. I went below for a smoke before taking up my bridge watch. Tomorrow would be Valentine's Day. There was a card on my desk. My heart leaped. I opened it. It was a valentine, home made. Its cover bore a drawing of Sugar Loaf Mountain, and the head and shoulders of a girl in a mantilla. The message was short and to the point.

"Your little Rio girl in blue, sends this Valentine to you,

What lovely moments we might have shared,

But for that sourpuss with the beard".

When I showed it to the Third Mate, he was not amused.

10
LEAVING TANKERS

The next ship I joined in North Shields, was to be my last oil tanker, I was by now thoroughly fed up with the dullness of peacetime trading at sea. At sea I was bored by the monotony of shipboard life, punctuated every fortnight or so by brief spells of frantic activity in port, loading or discharging. Each time we came into the Thames, which had become our regular home port, the Marine Superintendent came on board and cheerfully informed us that the *San Adolfo*, or some other ship, had cut her "turn-round" time by an hour, or maybe even two.

"Now then Captain, we'd like you to try and improve on that if you can" Naturally, the ship's company tried to do this. In the eight months I spent on *San Ambrosio* we cut our turn round from thirty seven hours to thirty one hours. I didn't have time to answer my mail. In 1948, the talk was of bigger, faster ships, with more powerful pumps. The American built T.2.s., the fast fifteen thousand tonners, built to beat the U-boats, proved their worth. Eagle had been given two in an effort to make up the fleet after the severe losses sustained.

They had the most ghastly names *Tresus* and *Turbinellus*, and were quickly nick-named the "Terrible Twins" for they discharged in the then phenomenal time of fifteen hours. I knew that tankers cost a lot of money to build and operate, and it is only economic when actually transporting oil. But, as far as I was personally concerned, the Company would have to find someone more willing to accept the conditions of life at sea than me to do my job.

San Ambrosio at that time was a "Lub-Oil" ship. She carried various grade of special lubricants for the motor industry, and machinery in general. She ran regular trips to the Gulf ports of the U.S.A., and once again I found myself visiting my old haunts of Houston,

Galveston, Port Arthur, Goose Creek and Norsworthy, all on the San Jacinto River or its estuary. The oils were loaded overall. Instead of being loaded through the ships pipelines they were loaded through flexibles of six inch diameter, whose ends were poked down the open tank hatches. All water and condensed moisture had to be rigorously excluded from tanks and pipelines, for it would discolour the oils. It was a mammoth task, this mopping up of the tank bottoms with "Tank flannel" and draining the last drop of water out of the intricate complex of a ship's pipeline system. We were heartily sick of pumprooms and lines by the time the shore supervisor declared himself satisfied. Still, it had to be done.

I had to admire the efficiency of the Americans at "Hooking up" a series of flexibles. Two men, using power winches and special clamps could set up a system, leading all over the decks to the tank hatches, in under an hour.

The oils which we knew as Spirax E.P.90, SAE 20, and so on, had much more glamorous names in American terminology. Names like Nevada Red, Texas Black. All the time it was a case of sampling, testing for water or discolouration. Now I have a car and appreciate how much care is taken by Oil companies. On one trip outward bound, the Captain decided to try to get rid of the cockroaches which infested the bridge accommodation. A supply of DDT smoke bombs had been put on board for the purpose. On a fine summer morning, we connected up the emergency steering gear on the poop. Arrangements were made for the midships to be evacuated, and the bombs were set off in various parts of the accommodation. All doors and ports were sealed. After about an hour, the wake of the ship began to look like a tortured snake. But the gyro compass repeater on the poop indicated the proper course.

"I wonder if the smoke from the bombs is affecting the master gyro" I said to the Captain.

"Surely not" he said. "But meanwhile go on the steering compass and we'll check." We watched carefully and found that the gyro compass was swinging regularly to one side then the other of the mean course.

As soon as the accommodation was cleared at four o'clock, I went into the gyro room. The Gyro compass was my special pet. As

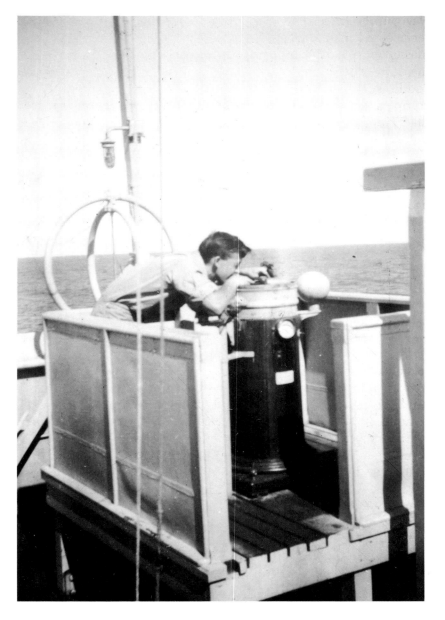

Taking a bearing on Monkey Island.

Navigating Officer it was my duty to see that it got the proper service and maintenance. I took off the cover and examined the master gyro carefully. Everything appeared to be in order. What the devil could it be? I made a last check of the air-vane, a delicate paddle system which transmitted the movements of the master compass to the repeaters in various parts of the ship. Ah, what was that? Tiny little whiskers between the aperture of the vane. I look it out into the light and examined it more closely. The aperture was blocked by a bunch of tiny crystals. I looked again at the master gyro. Through the sight window I could see its inner surface was coated with crystals. I realised that the heat of the spinning rotor had in some way crystallised the fumes from the bombs. This was confirmed when we found that a book left on a desk left its mark. All of the surfaces of the Cabins and alleyways had been given a deposit of fine crystals. It certainly killed the cockroaches, but it also had led to the demise of the gyro compass. For the next two to three days, I stripped the compass right down, cleaned every part of it, and restarted it. I did this three times, and every time the crystals reappeared. They were continually blown out of the rotor case as fast as I cleared them. Only a complete overhaul back at the factory would do the trick. For the rest of the trip we relied on the Magnetic compass. I relate this merely to show how things can happen at sea. Little things which of themselves are unimportant, but which building up on top of one another can be a cause of disaster. Suppose that, instead of fumigating in the open sea, we had tried it in the Channel. Before anyone might have noticed a wandering compass, the ship could have been ashore, or in collision with another vessel.

My last trip on *San Ambrosio* was up the Mississippi River to Baton Rouge. We took a full cargo all but two tanks, about 400 tons, in Goose Creek, then went round to South Pass, one of the channels of the mighty delta. The Mississippi River runs some 1700 miles through the heart of America, to pour its muddy outflow through the Delta into the Gulf of Mexico, it's a fascinating river to navigate. Our ship, a twelve thousand tonner, sailed 250 miles upstream, taking some two and a half days to do it. We had three pilots. The first, from sea through the Passes to Pilottown. The second, from

Pilottown for the eighty miles to New Orleans, and the third, from New Orleans to Baton Rouge. They were real Southerners, of French descent, Smoking innumerable seegars or chawin' tobacco, and regaling us with endless tales of the Mississippi.

For the entire length of the river from Baton Rouge to the sea, this mighty flood is contained between the Levees. These huge artificial banks, built to prevent flooding of the low-lying terrain on each side of the river, twist and turn for scores of miles as they follow the course of the river. At some points they are as much as half a mile from the water, the intervening space filled with dense scrub and trees growing on the rich alluvial soil. Real Huck Finn country. At other points the levees are the actual river banks, a hundred feet thick at the base. At New Orleans, for instance, the ship was above street level at the lower end of the city, the tops of the street cars just visible from our decks. Should a hydrogen bomb ever devastate the levees, untold miles of countryside rich and fertile would disappear beneath the waters of the Mississippi. The maintenance of these mighty banks and the conservancy of the river is carried out by the United States Army Engineers, whose vast fleet of vessels of every kind are to be found at work up and down the river.

There are few navigational marks in the lower reaches. The deep water is marked by a continuous line of driftwood, whole trees, logs and floating islands of brushwood sailed continually down on the current. All that the pilot did was keep the ship in the centre of this flotsam.

Above New Orleans we were delayed for six hours by fog. Since at that time we had no radar, we could only anchor. The local traders, however, did not stop for fog. By using the echo of their whistle from the banks, they could gauge their position in mid-stream. I had heard of this, but it was the first time I had seen it used. Very effective.

Baton Rouge is a fine modern city of approximately 200,000 people. It was close to Christmas and the shops and streets had an air of cheerful festivity about them. All very pleasant for those on shore, but for me it made only a feeling of nostalgia. Here was I thousands of miles from home. I would spend yet another Christmas at sea.

I gazed from the deck of the ship at the stark outline of the Huey Long Bridge which marks the limit for ocean going ships. Over to the East the tall buildings were already glowing with myriad lights in the December dusk. Thank God this would be my last trip. Let those who wanted to stay at sea. I had had enough.

Christmas was spent in Mid-Atlantic. The weather was not very good. We were travelling along with a depression, which was moving relatively only twenty miles an hour faster than the ship, and in roughly the same direction. Not that this was unusual. We frequently found ourselves keeping step with the weather systems of the Atlantic. Once, on the *San Felix*, we came home, all the way up the Channel, in beautiful Spring like weather, while the radio gave reports of snow and gales for all over England. It was only when we turned round the North Foreland and into the Thames Estuary that the fine weather fled before a screaming North Westerly storm, with a raging blizzard. As usual, the saloon was decorated for the occasion, and all the usual things were done. Singing Christmas Carols on the Eve of Christmas. Having a drink with the Master on Christmas Morning, and eating far too much.

On Boxing Day 1948 the weather worsened. Late in the afternoon the Captain altered course to East, True, in order to ease the ship's motion. Darkness fell and *San Ambrosio* plunged and rolled on her way, wallowing in the troughs of great seas like a drunken whale.

When I came on watch at midnight, the wind showed signs of shifting, with short fierce squalls of hail. The glass was starting to rise. By the middle of the watch the wind had veered to W.N.W. force nine. A heavy South Westerly swell was still running across the now North Westerly seas, making *San Ambrosio* take up that corkscrew motion beloved of all tanker men. Her decks could but rarely be seen beneath the white frothing tops of the waves as they continuously seethed aboard. This, I must impress, was normal enough in such conditions. I strode up and down, glancing occasionally at the Emerald glow of the Gyro repeater, to ensure the helmsman was keeping on course, and peering out of the windows into the streaming darkness.

San Ambrosio rolled heavily to port. Instead of returning, she lay rather longer in the trough than she should have. Perhaps because of the heavy swell catching her stern. Whatever the cause, it was disastrous. A huge green sea, its surface flecked with foam, engulfed first the port bow, then the entire port side. It seemed to move only slowly, but when its top struck the top bridge, I got some impression of its tremendous power. Automatically I glanced at the clock. Twenty past two. I found myself facing an appalling mass of water, deafened in its thunderous roar. Slowly the ship began to return upright, trembling in every rivet, under the awful weight of water. As she recovered I heard a lot of crashing and banging below decks. I checked the compass, but it was only five degrees off course. So it was not the fault of the helmsman that had allowed such a sea to board.

My next thought was the lookout man. He had been on Monkey Island because of the weather. Was he still there? I went outside in water up to my knees, splintered wood from the bulwarks banging against my legs.

"Smith Are you all right" I shouted.

"I – I think so, sir" he replied. "But the port lifeboat's gone".

I splashed round the corner. No, the boat was still there, but it was a wreck. A thirty foot steel motor lifeboat had been squeezed as by a giant hand and hung, disembowelled in its davits.

"Call the watch and the bosun to secure this mess" I said to Smith.

I turned to greet the Captain.

"Port boat is a write off sir".

"That's a detail, Stevenson. Go below and look at the accommodation".

It was a shambles. The port bulkhead of the deckhouse, behind which lay the Saloon and pantry, had taken the full force of the sea. Its top edge had been torn clean out of the rivets and bent inwards. The sea had burst the thick glass of two fifteen inch portholes to smithereens. We could find no piece larger than a marble. The water had shot across the saloon in two powerful jets and knocked down the plywood bulkhead separating the saloon from the cabin of the Third Mate, who had wakened from sleep to find himself drenched in cold seawater and his cabin in the shape of a "W". I found him stalking round the wreckage in pyjamas and seaboots, hair standing

Bay of Biscay.
Showing what a
giant sea can do
to a 36 foot
lifeboat.

on end and swearing horribly. Clouds of steam from broken radiator pipes and the pantry hot press obscured my vision. The smell of hot steam, wet carpets and furniture, mingled with the cold smell of the sea, brought in through the torn bulkhead by the gale. Stewards and sailors splashed through calf deep water, bailing out the sodden accommodation.

Over on the starboard side, which had escaped the water completely, the Mate slumbered on, blissfully unaware of the accident.

We sailed up the Manchester Ship Canal the first week in January 1949. As we passed through the locks, people out for their Sunday walk, pointed out to each other the damage on *San Ambrosio*.

"What did you bump into Mister?" a small boy called out.

"Nothing Son, Just a big sea".

His eyes popped.

The ship went to drydock in Birkenhead and I left her to go for my Master's Certificate. It was my farewell to tankers as a sea going officer.

My contract with Eagle expired in March. When they sent the renewal contract I had a lot to think about. I was going to get married after sitting my exams in June. It seemed so easy. By signing that paper I could look forward to security, steady if slow promotion and an excellent pension.

Against this I could also look forward to poignant farewells and long months of separation from my wife. I would return to a cheerless oil jetty in some god-forsaken oil depot, to find her waiting with other officers' wives, half frozen and miserable. We would spend twenty-four hours together continually interrupted by the numerous demands placed on an officer in port. News of home would mean little to me, who would know it only as a place to spend a leave. My fiancée had been in the WRNS and knew something of the conditions of sharing a sailor's life. To her credit she did not influence me in any way. The decision was to be mine.

At the end of March, I resigned from the oil company to become an unemployed officer, studying for Master. I was not alone, as I discovered when I applied at the Labour Exchange in Leith. There were so many of us that on "Dole" days, they made a special queue for the college boys, so that they could get to school on time.

In early June I found myself with a brand new foreign-going Master's Certificate and no job. I had a little money, sufficient to get married in August. I went to the Rehabilitation Bureau in Drumsheugh Gardens, Edinburgh. This office had been set up to find employment for ex-service officers. I hoped they could do something for me. The official I met was very polite. He even offered me a cup of tea. But he did not offer me a suitable job. In my own profession I was a skilled man, but out of it I was just another fellow with a reasonably good education. The jobs he mentioned were reasonably good too. Salesman with a shoe firm, road foreman, trainee manager. Again salesman. I visualised myself trying to sell fire extinguishers. With my temperament I had a shrewd idea that if I got too many refusals I was likely to empty one over the unfortunate customer's head.

It seemed hopeless. I began to visit the offices of shipping companies in Leith and Glasgow looking for a coastal job. Currie Line of Leith offered me a second mate's berth on a new ship, then being completed in Dundee. I accepted tentatively. I did not have to join her till the end of August.

One day I met my old friend Bob Kirk, home on leave from Abadan.

"Well, how goes it, David?" he asked. I told him. He was not impressed.

"What about the tugs in Abadan?" he asked. "I know a few of the Tug lads and they seem to enjoy life".

"Abadan!" I said. "No fear, Bob. I had enough of that place to last me a lifetime".

"Now, not so fast, Young Steve" said Bob. "There are a lot of new, air-conditioned houses going up. Some of the Tug Masters have their families out there. After a year you can have your wife out too. And, some of the tugs are air-conditioned. I know that for a fact".

I paused to think. Now I did remember that the tugs in Abadan were kept very smart and clean. All they did was pull tankers off the jetties and hare back to their moorings. It could not all be like that, of course, but, definitely, the picture of life as a tug master in the Gulf, began to look better.

"I'll talk to Joyce about it" I said.

"Bring her along and have a yarn with the wife" said Bob.

Joyce, while disliking the initial separation of twelve months, was enthusiastic enough, after listening to Bob and Chris expound on life in Abadan. Our main concern was that we would be together.

I wrote to British Tanker Company, and was invited for interview. Immediately I was offered a Chief Officer's berth in the tanker fleet, with promise of Command in five years. I turned this most generous offer down flat.

"If you can't give me a job on the tugs, sir, there's no use continuing this interview" I said firmly. "Had I wanted tanker life, I would never have left Eagle."

"All right, Mr. Stevenson" said the Marine Superintendent, "You'll get your tug. Only the London Office wanted you to be a tanker officer".

On 6th September, with my new bride, I went through to Port Glasgow to join, as Chief Officer, a ship called *Suilven*. She was lying at Lamont's Yard, fitting out for her new role of Pilot Cutter for the Khor Musa Bar, in the Persian Gulf.

Suilven was the last of the big steam yachts in the Clyde. Build in 1924, as "Thalassa" by John Brown's, Clydebank, for an American millionaire (Eugene Higgins) she was the last word in luxury. But when I got aboard, I found that, though a comfortable little ship, all her lovely panelled lounges, save for the main saloon, were being divided into cabins for pilots. Plywood bulkheads cut at random through graceful plaster cornices. On deck her spacious after deck was occupied by two MOT lifeboats and a couple of motor pilot launches.

Still, the day of the big private yacht of her type was going, and she would make a fine pilot cutter.

She was to sail under the flag of Iran, under British Tanker Management. I went in search of a crew at the local Shipping Office. The clerk at the engagement counter was brusque.

"*Suilven*, eh? That's the Iranian Flag ship. Well, Mister, the only way you'll get a crew for her is to go up the cemetery and dig them up".

"Surely you have men on the Pool here?" I asked.

The *Suilven*, built as a private yacht in 1924 and converted to a pilot cutter in the Gulf.

"Sure we have, but hardly enough to man our own ships".

I had to take what offered from the local grapevine. At that time, the shortage of good sailors was acute and a man had to be bad to be put off the Merchant Navy Pool. When I had interviewed a few I realised what I was in for. Everyone had a bad discharge in his book. One had only recently left prison. After several days, I gathered what I judged to be the best of a bad lot.

On the Saturday, I bade my wife goodbye. I would not see her for at least a year. On a fine Sunday morning we slipped out of the basin and headed down the Clyde. I gazed at the hills of Arran and astern to the Mountains of Argyll. I felt a sharp pang of regret. Had I, by leaving Eagle tankers, merely jumped from the frying pan into the fire? I had my doubts.

Bill Scource, Suilven's captain was a big jovial man. He was a senior tug master in Abadan on leave when the chance of taking the yacht back to the Gulf had been offered to him. His wife was with him on this trip. A slim, quiet lady, she was the antithesis of big burly Bill. Yet they got on famously together. Bill's idea was to make a pleasure trip out of the voyage to Abadan.

"It's not every day that I get the chance to act the part of a ruddy millionaire, with my own yacht" he remarked. "Now let's have a look at the charts and see where we'll put in for bunkers and water".

We finally decided on Oran, Port Said, Aden and Abadan.

"Always wanted to have a look round North Africa and Egypt" enthused Bill. "For all the time I spent on tankers, I never got ashore at Port Said".

As the little white hulled yacht sailed down the Irish Sea, it looked as if the trip would indeed be a pleasant one. The crew, in spite of their bad references, appeared to be settling down.

About a week later, after a good crossing of the Bay, we reached Oran and berthed round breakfast time. Bill and his wife set off ashore for the day.

"I'll be back about teatime, Steve" he said. "Once the stores have arrived, why don't you take a run ashore yourself?"

"I might just do that" I smiled. "Have a good time".

Within the hour, all thoughts of going ashore had fled. The crew were roaring drunk on the local fire water, a vicious brandy, exchanged with the hordes of Arab merchants on the quay. I had an idea the crew would make an attempt to swop ship's stores for more hooch. In order to foil this we three officers kept watch on deck and overside. I telephoned the Agent.

"Will you please tell Captain Scource his crew are paralytic drunk, and he'd be better to return on board as soon as he can" I said.

As the bunker and water hoses were being taken off, Bill came on board.

"What's the trouble, Mate?" he asked.

I waved my hand around the decks. Staggering, falling, or collapsed in drunken heaps, were the members of our gallant crew.

Within half an hour we were at sea. The officers had let go the moorings and taken over the steering and lookout duties.

Oran was blue haze on the starboard quarter by four o'clock. The Captain and I were on the bridge, talking over the events of the day, when the Chief Engineer rushed up on deck, his eyes staring in fright.

"Captain" he gasped. "The chief steward's run amok and he's carving up the fourth engineer with a galley knife".

Both of us dashed below. Leaning, white-faced against the doorway of the pantry, the young Fourth clutched his left arm. Blood dripped from two great slashes across his forearm.

"I was just kidding him about the grub" he whispered, "Then he went for me with a knife".

In the struggle the engineer had grabbed for the knife, missed the handle, and had grabbed instead, the razor sharp blade of the knife.

"Where's the Steward now?" asked Bill.

"Wandering round the ship somewhere. He's still got the knife sir".

"Right" Bill gestured to the others who had gathered round. "Take this lad to my cabin. I'll be along in a minute" He turned to me.

"Steve, take the port side – I'll take Starboard. When you see him, hit him as hard as you can".

I went round the port side, grabbing up my steel cased torch from my cabin as I passed. Neither coward nor hero, I hoped devoutly that Bill would meet the Steward first.

Through the Chinese Library, past the gangway door. There was no sign of the man. As I entered the saloon I saw him. He had his back to me, gibbering and slavering at the grim figure of the Captain as he advanced, hand outstretched for the weapon.

"Give me that knife" Bill said.

I tiptoed closed ready to strike.

"Take a look behind you" said Bill, "the mate's at your back".

The man glanced quickly behind him. For all he was a big man the skipper moved like a cat. The Steward went down like a log.

"Lock him in a stateroom Steve" said Bill. "Make sure you leave nothing in the room that will hurt him when he comes to."

When the Steward recovered, he had no recollection of the fact that he had attacked someone. It had been a brainstorm, induced by the potent fumes of North African Brandy.

The next thing was to stitch up the wounded engineer. With the first aid kit, and the Ship Captain's Medical guide, we put fifteen stitches in the arm. The fingers we bound up as best we could. We put both the engineer and steward ashore in Malta for repatriation, and pushed on for Port Said.

In Port Said it was the same story. The officers guarding the ship from the depredations of the crew. Fortunately, as soon as we bunkered we got a pilot and set off down the canal. On the way we met a convoy of big laden tankers, but thanks to the handiness of Suilven and the skill of the pilot, we passed all twelve and anchored in the Bitter Lakes for the night.

Our next port was Aden, reached after ten days of stifling heat. It was the Crews' last chance to do any thieving for barter, but they were foiled again.

We had so much trouble with the crew for the entire voyage. Insolence, refusal to carry out any but the most essential tasks. And a sullen, burning resentment at the authority which had so far balked them from the rich pickings to be made from the sale of the yacht's stores. For the insolence, the Captain had a simple remedy. He issued instructions to all the officers that at the slightest hint of insubordination the man had to be reported. This was recorded in the log, together with a fine of five shillings.

I was doubtful of the efficacy of this, but Bill said,

"Look Mr. Mate, all we can do is fine them. I know five bob isn't much, but a lot of five bobs can soon mount up. When we get to Abadan these cowboys are in for a shock"

Twenty eight days out from Port Glasgow, Suilven tied up to the Buoys off Bawarda, Abadan. It had been for me a nightmare voyage. It was the first and only time in my career at sea that I had to lock my door when I turned in. Even when I went on watch I locked it, in case someone stole my personal effects. The feeling that the officers were looked upon by a hostile crew as fair game, that the very ship they sailed on was for them some kind of prey, was for me something new in my experience.

At the pay off, held in the British Vice Consul's Office, which did duty as a Shipping Office, Captain Scource's loggings bore fruit. So many and so frequent had been the fines, that almost every man, certainly the worst, owed the ship money. Their twenty eight days of sailing was not enough, after normal deductions had been made, to pay the fines. Tolwar, the Vice Consul, a big, dignified Indian, spoke to the first man.

"Rafferty? Your balance of wages is Four pounds ten".

"Okay. Give me the bloody money and let me get the hell out of this place"

Rafferty's voice was truculent.

"Just a moment" Tolwar's voice hardened. "You owe Captain Scource seven pounds in fines".

"Aye, Ah do. But the fines is always cancelled at the end of the trip".

A tinge of apprehension was evident in Rafferty's manner Tolwar's eyebrows lifted.

"Indeed? What have you to say to this, Captain?"

Bill looked up innocently from the papers he was studying.

"What's that sir? Oh the fines? They stand as they are".

There was immediate uproar. What Bill was sentencing the majority of the crew to, was in effect, another voyage on a tanker out East. If a man owed the company money for any reason, he had to sign on another ship to work it off. It was the only way to clear his debt.

In one fell afternoon's work, we got our crowd of scallywags signed on, each man to a different ship, and all bound for Australia,

India, Singapore or some far off place. It seemed a rotten trick in a way, but I could not find in me to feel sorry for them. They had been the cause of a man's brain becoming temporarily unhinged, they had caused another to be severely wounded. They had made a hell out of what could have been a pleasant trip for all hands.

As they left the ship, I stood at the gangway to see them off. "Best of luck, boys" I said. "Where you're going, you'll need it". The language was unprintable.

*   *   *

AFTERMATH

From 1951 to 1952 I became a tug master in the fleet of fine sea-going tugs based in Abadan but working all over the Persian Gulf as it was called at the time. But due to Iran taking over the Anglo Iranian Oil Company and British Oil Company, I moved back to England and the rest of my life could be another story, as it related to cross-channel ferries, marine management, piloting ships in various ports of the world and being Harbour Master of the small but historic North Yorkshire port of Whitby.

THE BATTLE OF THE ATLANTIC
50 YEARS ON

In the town of Altenbruch in spring 1993 a re-union of sailors from countries which had fought the bitter campaign of the North Atlantic in World War 2 took place.

Several thousand ill-equipped mostly elderly and vulnerable ships attempted to keep Britain supplied with food and the materials of war. In one convoy alone for example, out of fifty-four ships, thirty were sunk. It was a "Turkey Shoot". Many of the men who took part both British and German were little more than boys eighteen years upwards (I was seventeen) with little knowledge of the sea. Never mind fighting on it. The recollection of Karl Wahnig a stoker rating on U-802 "Messdecks slippery with oil, old food and vomit. The entire boat reeking of sweat and unwashed bodies, cabbage water, ersatz coffee and foul air". Similarly, messdecks in a Corvette or Destroyer – sick and food swilling around in six inches or so of cold salt water which you jumped into from your hammock.

Recollections of a survivor from a torpedoed vessel "The tremendous ear shattering bang of explosions, the acrid smell of cordite reaching into your lungs, the stomach churning fear of imminent death. Fire, flames and smoke. The yells and screams of trapped ship-mates. The relatively orderly scramble as we practised many times to get the boats lowered and away." Over and above the darkness and the dreadful freezing cold, the final awesome sinking of the ship with the eerie screech and whistle of air being pushed up through the air vents and ventilators from all the holes and 'tween decks, all gave the last agonising gasp of the ship as she died. At one stage U-boats were sinking 350,000 tons per month, an unsustainable amount of tonnage. In all of this the dying of shivering oil-soaked survivors after many days of misery.

Plymouth had been the main naval H.Q. for fighting the war. Churchill changed the main H.Q. to Liverpool, as he thought that Plymouth was too vulnerable for invasion. Liverpool was a fine seaport strategically placed to receive all marine traffic from America in its large extensive dock system and aided by Manchester with its magnificent canal and docks. Derby House was chosen and its deep basement strengthened to withstand a direct hit of a 500lb. bomb. Admiral sir Percy Noble set up "Western Approaches Command" under Admiral Maxwell Horton.

INDEX OF SHIPS